G. Dallas (George Dallas) Lind

Lessons in Physiology for Beginners

G. Dallas (George Dallas) Lind

Lessons in Physiology for Beginners

ISBN/EAN: 9783744649858

Printed in Europe, USA, Canada, Australia, Japan

Cover: Foto ©Thomas Meinert / pixelio.de

More available books at **www.hansebooks.com**

LESSONS IN PHYSIOLOGY
FOR BEGINNERS

INCLUDING

BRIEF AND PLAIN DESCRIPTIONS OF THE MOST
IMPORTANT PARTS OF THE HUMAN BODY
AND THE ACTION OF ALCOHOL
AND OTHER STIMULANTS

BY

GEORGE D. LIND, M.D.
AUTHOR OF " LESSONS IN PHYSIOLOGY," ETC.

DANVILLE, INDIANA
INDIANA PUBLISHING COMPANY
1897

AUTHOR'S PREFACE.

———∘∘ͦ∘ͦ∘∘———

To write a book for beginners in any branch of knowledge is no easy task. The author realizes the difficulties in the way, and freely admits his inability to produce a *perfect* work in this line. Years of experience, however, in teaching Physiology to all grades of pupils, from the child of ten years to the medical student of twenty-five, have qualified him, in part, for a task of this kind. Therefore, without further apology, this little book is submitted to the public to stand on its intrinsic merits.

The author believes that the following lessons will not only interest boys and girls and lead them to a further study of this important subject, but will help them to form habits in youth that stand for health and strength of body and mind in manhood and womanhood.

GEORGE D. LIND.

St. Louis, U.S.A., April, 1892.

TABLE OF CONTENTS.

[This table is not intended for reference, but merely to show at a glance the general nature of the subjects discussed. For ready reference to any particular part see Alphabetical Index at close of volume.]

LESSONS IN PHYSIOLOGY

FOR BEGINNERS.

———•o:•:oo———

LESSON 1.

Introduction.

[NOTE. — This lesson may be simply read as an exercise, and not assigned for study, if the teacher think proper.]

1. What is Physiology? — You have already, no doubt, some idea of the meaning of the word. You suppose it is in some way connected with a knowledge of the human body. You have seen the word **Anatomy**. It means the study of the *parts of the body,* how it is put together, and what it is made of. The word **Physiology** is properly applied to a knowledge of how the *parts of the body act,* or the working of the machine, if we may so call the body. The word **Hygiene** has also probably met your eyes. It refers to the art of *taking care of the body* and preserving its health. For the sake of simplicity we generally call the study of Anatomy, Physiology, and Hygiene by one name, — " Physiology."

2. A Bit of History. — The ancients knew very little about the human body. Hippocrates lived 400 years before the birth of Christ, and because he knew a little about bones and muscles and advised the sick, he was called the " Father of Medicine "; but in a few months of study you may be able to know a great deal that Hip-

1

pocrates did not know. For many hundreds of years very little was added to the knowledge of Hippocrates. In the year 1619 William Harvey, an English surgeon, first discovered that the blood made a complete circuit of the body. Since that time progress in knowledge has been gradual and rapid, and to-day a great deal is known about the human body in health and in disease, and as a result of this knowledge human life has been prolonged and disease is not so terrible as it once was.

3. **Cells.** — Not only human bodies, but the bodies of all animals and the substance of all plants, — that is, **all living things,** — are made up of very minute parts called *cells*. A cell is usually so small that a high power of the microscope is necessary to see it at all, but some cells are quite large and can be seen by the unaided eye. Millions upon millions of these tiny things are required to make up an ordinary human body. New cells grow from old cells, and in this way the body increases in size. Cells are in various shapes. Some are round, some flat, some drawn out into long threads. The different kinds of cells joined together in different ways form the different kinds of **tissue,** as any particular part of the body is called. Thus we have bony tissue, which is hard and solid; nerve tissue, which is soft; muscular tissue, which is soft and in threads very close together; fibrous tissue, which is firmer and very tough and elastic.

4. **Organs.** — The word organ as used in Physiology means any part of the body that does a special kind of work, as the stomach is the main organ of digestion, the heart of circulation, and so on. If we were to compare a human body to a house, we might say that the *materials,* — that is, the stone, brick, wood, sand, glass, iron, etc. —

which go to make up the house are the *tissues,* while the doors, windows, roof, walls, etc., are the *organs* of the house.

5. **Systems.** — When several organs act together to perform a common work, we speak of them as forming a system. Thus all parts which aid in preparing the food taken together form the *digestive system,* those which circulate the blood the circulatory system, and so on. In this book these terms will not be frequently used.

6. **The Composition of the Body.** — To understand exactly what the body is composed of would require a study of the science of Chemistry. Some time in the future you will study this science, and then you will have a better understanding of Physiology. Certain facts must at first be learned, although we may not understand them thoroughly. If we were to say that three-fourths of the human body was water you would scarcely comprehend it : yet such is a scientific fact. Water can be so combined with other substances that its identity is lost, and it is only by careful chemical experiments that it can be separated and its existence proven.

—◦◦—

LESSON 2.

Dry Bones.

1. **What are Bones ?** — Every child knows something about bones. You know that they are the hard parts of the higher animals. It is easy to see that they are the solid framework around which softer and more yielding parts are built. But let us learn a little more about

bone by making a careful examination of any dry bone
we may chance to pick up.   We may find it more inter-

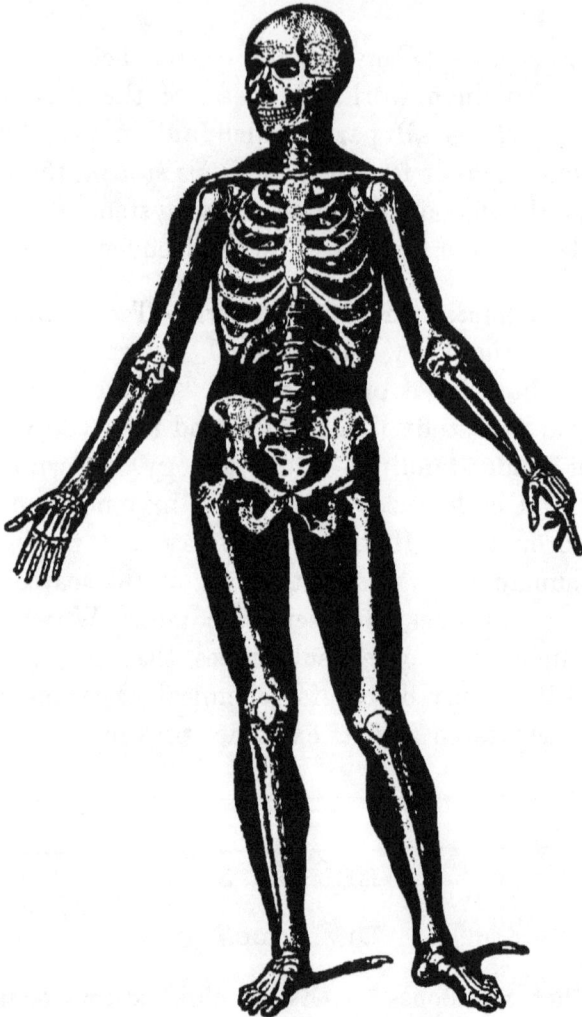

FIG. 1.

esting than we at first might suppose.   Strike it on the
table.   It is hard and solid.   Hit it with a hammer a

very hard blow. It breaks more easily than ordinary wood, yet perhaps not so easily as a piece of rock of the same size and shape. Try to break it with your hands. If it be a long, slender bone you will perhaps be able to do it, but if it be fresh from an animal, it will bend before it will break. It has a certain degree of brittleness and yet a certain degree of elasticity.

2. **Structure of Bone.** — Examine the broken fragment. If it be of a long, round bone, the outside will be seen to be of a solid and compact nature and the central part a cavity. Near the enlarged end, you will observe that it is full of small holes, or cavities, throughout, with only a thin shell of compact bone on the outside. If it be a flat or irregular bone, this sponge-like appearance will be in the center, and a wall of compact bone on the outside. Make a collection of old, dry bones of any animal or animals, and break some of them in different places, and compare their appearances. Human bones are almost exactly similar in structure to the bones of domestic animals.

3. **Composition of Bone.** — Put a bone into a hot fire and leave it until it becomes perfectly white; when cool, observe that it has lost much in weight but yet has the same bulk and shape, and the appearance is the same except that it is whiter. Strike it gently and observe that it breaks much more easily than one that has not been burned. It is no longer tough and strong, but brittle and fragile. Something has been removed by the fire. Now, if you put a bone in a weak acid and let it remain several days, and examine it, you will find that it has lost some in weight and is soft enough to be readily bent double and even tied in a knot if long enough, but otherwise its nat-

ure and appearance are the same.   The acid has removed
something.

The fire has removed the gelatine, or animal matter,
which gives it toughness and elasticity.   The acid has
removed the mineral, or earthy, matter, which gives it
firmness and solidity.   The chemist tells us that about
one-third of the bone is gelatine and two-thirds mineral
matter.

4. **Young and Old Bones.**— The bones of young animals
contain in proportion more of the soft gelatine, and are
therefore more easily bent; while the bones of full-grown
and old animals contain in proportion more earthy matter,
and are therefore more solid and brittle.   Nature arranges
this just right.   The young animal is lighter and more
active.   The bones have less weight to bear and are not
so liable to be bent, and can therefore be more elastic, thus
permitting greater activity.   The old animal is heavier,
and the bones must be firmer to bear the weight.   It is
less active and more careful in its movements, and the
bones are less liable to be broken.   What is true of animals
is true of the human body.   It would not do for children
to have the brittle bones of old people, nor for old people
to have the yielding bones of children.

5. **The Marrow.**— The long bones of young animals
contain a reddish, fatty-like substance in their center we
call **marrow**.   It consists of fat and blood vessels.   In old
animals this marrow is yellow and consists mostly of fat.
In the young and growing bone it helps to nourish the
bone by supplying blood.

6. **Bone under the Microscope.**— It is to be hoped your
teacher, or some one, will be able to show you a slice of
bone under the microscope.   If not, the picture will give

you a pretty good idea of how it appears when ground down very thin and highly magnified. By comparing cross and longitudinal sections it can be seen that numerous minute channels run through the bone in various directions. The large, whitish spots in the picture are these channels cut across. These are called *Haversian canals*, from the man who first discovered them. Numerous dark spots, with dark lines running in all directions from them, appear arranged in circles around the canals. These spots are the cavities of bone cells and are called *lacunæ*, a word meaning " little lakes." The lines are little channels branching off from the cells, and are called *canaliculi* (" little canals").

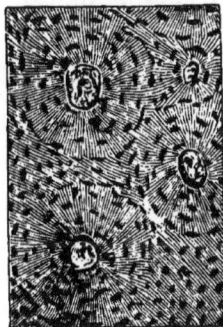

FIG. 2.

In the living bone these cavities and tubes are filled with the thin part of the blood, which brings the material for the growth of the bone.

7. How Bones Grow. — Bones are at first composed of a soft substance called *cartilage*. They gradually become harder by a disappearance of the cartilage cells, which are replaced by bone cells. This change from cartilage to bone is very gradual, beginning at certain points in a bone and increasing all around these points until nearly the entire bone is solidified. This is not completed in some bones until late in life. Bones also increase in size as the animal gets larger. When bones are broken in a healthy animal, a substance pours out from the broken ends, and if they be brought together, in a short time new bone will form between the ends and firmly join the pieces into one again.

8. Coverings of Bones. — All bones are covered except at their ends with a thin membrane, which is made up mostly of small blood vessels. From this membrane the bone gets its blood for its nourishment. If you get a fresh bone from a young animal, you may be able to peel off this membrane with the aid of a knife. It is called the **per-i-os-te-um** (around bone).

LESSON 3.

The Uses of Bones.

1. The Framework of the Body. — Bones form the framework around and within which the softer parts are arranged and kept in position. Without the bones the body would be a shapeless mass. They form a movable framework, which is capable of being folded and placed in many different positions. This framework is called the **skel-e-ton** (hard).

2. They Protect the Delicate Parts. — The brain is a soft, delicate mass of cells; the lungs are a fine network of soft material; the liver is a mass of soft cells; the eye is a fine piece of mechanism; the ear contains minute bodies, which would easily be destroyed if exposed. All these and other important parts are surrounded and *protected by bones*.

3. They Aid Motion. — The muscles which move the parts of the body and the body itself from place to place would be entirely useless without the bones, which form solid points of attachment for them. They also act as levers for the muscles.

4. Bones of Animals Useful to Man. — Many useful and ornamental articles may be cut from bone. When ground to a fine powder, they make the best fertilizer for growing crops the farmer can use. Phosphorus and other chemicals used in the arts and in medicine are made from bones. Bone-black, or animal charcoal, which is used for making shoe-blacking, for painting, and to purify sugar, is made from bones.

LESSON 4.

The Bones of Our Bodies.

[NOTE. — The teacher should not require pupils to memorize the names of the bones, but by frequent reference to them most of them will be learned.]

1. **Number of Bones.** — There are two hundred bones in a human body. This does not include the teeth, which are not properly called bones, nor the very minute bones in the internal ear. Imagine a line to pass through the body from the crown of the head to a point between the feet. Nearly in this line will be found thirty-four single bones. The remaining one hundred and sixty-six bones are arranged in pairs, one on each side of the body.

2. **The Names of the Bones.** — Not only has every bone in the body a name, but all the principal grooves and projections and openings in each bone have names. These names are from the Latin and Greek languages, and were given to the bones when these languages were the principal ones used by scholars. They may sound foreign to us at first, but you can soon become familiar with many of them.

3. The Bones of the Head. — There are twenty-two bones in the head. All taken together form the skull. The skull is composed of the **cra-ni-um,** or that part that

FIG. 3.

encloses the brain, and the **face**. There are eight bones in the cranium, firmly joined so as to form a box in which the brain lies perfectly protected from injury.

Here are the names of the bones of the cranium : —

The **Frontal** (front): forms the forehead.

The **Oc-cip-i-tal** (back of head) : forms back and lower part.

The **Sphe-noid** (wedge-like): forms the base.

The **Eth-moid** (sieve-like) : between eye cavities.

Two **Tem-po-ral** : one on each side below.

Two **Pa-ri-e-tal** (a wall) : one on each side above.

There are fourteen bones in the face : —

Two **Na-sal** (nose): form the " bridge " of the nose.

Two **Ma-lar** (cheek) : below eye cavities.

Two **Lach-ry-mal** (a tear): inner corner of eye cavities.

Two **Pal-ate** : form back part of roof of mouth.

Two **Inferior tur-bi-nated** (scroll-like): in nose cavities.

Two **Superior max-il-la-ry** (jaw bone): the upper jaw.

Vo-mer (plow-share) : between nose cavities.

Inferior max-il-la-ry : the lower jaw.

4. **Bones of the Trunk, or Body Proper.** — There are fifty-eight bones in the trunk, forming three groups: the **thorax**, or chest ; the **spinal column,** or backbone ; and the **pelvis,** or hips.

There are twelve pairs of **ribs.** The upper or first seven pairs are joined to the sternum in front by separate short pieces of cartilage and are called the *true ribs.* The other five pairs are called *false ribs.* The two last pairs are not joined to the sternum and are called *floating ribs.* The other three pairs have their cartilages united to each other, and the upper one to the seventh rib. All are joined to the spinal column.

The **Ster-num** (hard), or breastbone.

Two **Clav-i-cles** (key), or collar-bones.

Two **Scap-u-las** (spade), or shoulder-blades.

The ribs, sternum, clavicles, and scapulas together form

the *thorax*, which is a kind of cage, enclosing and protecting the heart, lungs, and other organs.

The *spinal column* is a column of twenty-four bones, called **ver-te-bræ** (singular *ver-te-bra*, that which turns). Each vertebra is a round mass of bone with projections, some of which form a ring; and when all are together these rings form a channel called the *spinal canal*. In this channel lies, perfectly protected, the spinal cord, an important part of the nervous system. The first or upper vertebra is called the **at-las**, from the name of a heathen god, who was supposed to support the earth on his shoulders. The second is called the **ax-is**, or pivot. When you move the head up and down, as in bowing, the occipital bone of the head glides on the atlas. When you turn your head from side to side, the atlas turns around the axis.

The first seven vertebræ are called **cer-vi-cal** (of the neck). The next twelve are called **dor-sal** (of the back), and the last five are called **lum-bar** (of the loins).

The **pel-vis** (a basin) is formed by the two **in-nom-i-na-ta** (nameless) bones; the **sa-crum** (sacred) bone, which is really a continuation of the spinal column; and the **coc-cyx** (cuckoo), a small bone attached to the end of the sacrum.

Fig. 4.

The **os hy-oi-des** (u-shaped) is a small bone at the root of the tongue, having many muscles attached to it.

5. The Bones of the Upper Limbs. — Each upper limb contains thirty bones:

The **hu-me-rus** (arm): the long bone of the upper arm.

The **ul-na:** ⎫
The **ra-di-us:** ⎭ bones of the forearm.

The **car-pus** (wrist): eight small bones arranged in two rows.

Beginning with the side the thumb is on the bones of the upper or row next the arm are as follows: **scaph-oid** (boat-shaped); **sem-i-lu-nar** (half moon); **cu-ne-i-form** (wedge-shaped); **pi-si-form** (pea-shaped). Beginning next the thumb, in the second or row next the hand they are: **tra-pe-zi-um**; **trap-e-zoid**; **os mag-num** (large bone); **un-ci-form** (hook like).

The **met-a-car-pus** (beyond the carpus), or bones of the hand, five in number.

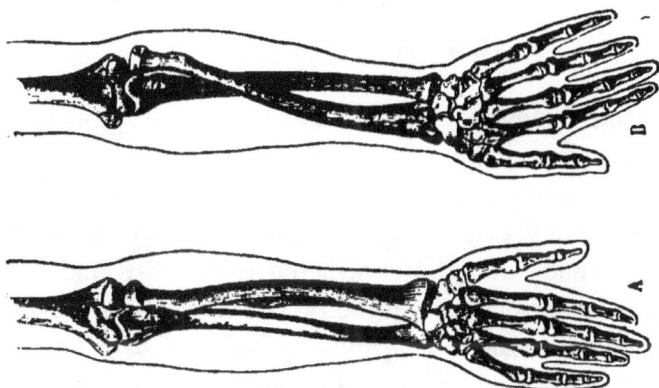

Fig. 5.

The **pha-lan-ges** (rows of soldiers), fourteen in number, three to each finger and two to the thumb.

6. Bones of the Lower Limbs. — Each lower limb has thirty bones:

The **fe-mur** (thigh): the bone of the thigh, or upper leg, the longest and heaviest bone in the body.

The **tib-i-a** (flute): the large bone of the leg proper, the "shin bone."

The **fib-u-la** (a brace): the small bone of the leg.

The **pa-tel-la** (a small pan): the knee cap.

The **tar-sus** (ankle): seven small bones.

The largest is the **os cal-cis**, or heel bone; the **as-trag-a-lus** (a die) joins the ankle to the leg; the **cu-boid** (cube-shaped); the **scaph-oid**; the internal, middle, and external **cu-ne-i-form**.

The **met-a-tar-sus** (beyond the tarsus), or bones of the foot, five in number.

The **pha-lan-ges** correspond to the phalanges of the hand.

LESSON 5.

How to Care for Our Bones.

1. Our Bones are Alive. — Although the bones we have been experimenting with are simply dead matter, like sticks and stones, we must bear in mind that the bones in our bodies are living things. The blood circulates through them, and they are being torn down and rebuilt, as all other tissues of the body are. *Constant pressure on a bone will cause it to grow crooked, just as a young tree may be made to grow crooked by binding it to a stake. The weight of the body tends to bend the bones in young children, and by walking too soon they frequently become bow-legged.*

2. Bones Need Nourishment. — We shall learn after a while that the body is kept in a proper state by the nourishment afforded by the blood, and the blood gets its nourishment from the food we eat. The bones require a constant supply of nourishment suitable to their nature. Good food in proper quantities, and all the conditions which favor proper digestion of the food, and circulation of the blood are necessary to have healthy and perfect bones. *Alcoholic drinks disturb the digestion and tend to diminish the nourishing qualities of the blood, and therefore indirectly affect the growth and condition of bones.* Some professional beggars are so cruel as to give their children whiskey or gin, to stunt their growth and make them puny and sickly-looking, that they may excite the compassion of those from whom they beg. *This illustrates the effect of alcohol on the bones.*

3. **Tight Clothing.** — The Chinese much admire small feet in women, and sometimes the parents bind the feet of their children when very young so that they cannot grow. A horrible deformity is produced, sometimes so great that the person is unable to walk. Our fashionable people frequently deform their feet by crowding them into shoes too small for them. School girls often foolishly try to produce a small waist by wearing a tightly laced corset. The ribs are made to grow inward, and the organs within the chest are crowded for room. *Much suffering later in life is the consequence of such absurd conduct. Clothing should never be tight. The bones should have freedom to grow in a natural way.*

4. **Unnatural Positions.** — Pupils in school often acquire habits of leaning or bending over their desks until there is actual deformity in the shoulders and spinal column. *Round, or stoop, shoulders are always caused by careless habits. Always sit or stand erect, taking care to keep the shoulders back.*

5. *Old persons* are more liable to have broken bones, as their bones are more brittle ; therefore they should be careful to avoid all causes of falling. *Children* should not be

lifted by the arms, nor placed on their feet too soon before they are able to walk. Their bones are easily bent.

6. *Fresh air, sunshine, cleanliness, wholesome food and drink, exercise, and avoidance of exposure to extreme cold and to dampness, are all necessary for a perfectly healthy condition of the bony framework.*

LESSON 6.

The Joints.

1. The Perfect Machine.—The human body is like a perfect piece of machinery. There is a good reason for having so many bones, or pieces, in the skeleton. This gives a great variety of motions. Observe how many positions the hand and fingers are capable of taking, and how many kinds of motions may be made with them. This would not be possible if the framework were not in so many pieces. The body is not only perfectly adapted to many motions and positions, but it is a very strong machine, not easily put out of repair by use. The numerous pieces of the skeleton are firmly and perfectly joined together, in some places permitting much motion, in others very little, according as the necessity exists.

2. Parts of a Joint.—To form a movable joint, the following parts are necessary : the edges or ends of two bones, *ligaments, cartilage, synovial membrane, and synovia.*

3. Ligaments.—These are bands or cords of fibrous tissue, elastic, pliable, and very tough, which bind the ends of the bones together in a manner similar to strap hinges on a door. Some pass from one bone to another across the joint, others completely surround the joint as with a cap. You may readily point out the ligaments in a joint from the leg of an ox or sheep, as you find it in the butcher's shop. Try cutting one with a knife, and observe how very tough they are. Try to pull a joint apart ; you cannot do it, so strong are the ligaments which hold it together. Ligaments are not well supplied with blood, and when stretched or partly torn, as in a sprained ankle, they are a long time in healing. One should be careful in jumping over fences, running on uneven ground, and in play, lest a sprained ankle be the result.

4. **Cartilage.** — In all movable joints the ends of the two bones are covered with a thin layer of a pearly white substance, very smooth and firm, yet much softer than bone. This is permanent cartilage, that is, cartilage that never changes to bone. It acts as a cushion to lessen the jar or shock that would occur in walking, running, or leaping. Between the vertebræ there is a separate piece of fibro-cartilage (a kind containing fibers). The weight of the body during the day compresses these cartilages ; and at night, when lying down, they regain their original condition. A little flattening of each of these cartilages amounts to nearly half an inch in all of them, so that a man is really half an inch taller in the morning than he is in the evening. These cartilages in the backbone permit a considerable bending of the spinal column, each one yielding just a little.

5. **A Joint is Self-oiling.** — In all machinery, wherever one part slides or moves on another there would be much wear, and more power would be required to move the parts, if they were not frequently oiled. In the body nature has provided for this by a beautiful contrivance.

A membrane covers each movable joint inside of the l̄ aments. This membrane secretes, that is manufactures, and pours out a slippery, transparent fluid, called **syn-o-vi-a,** or " joint-water." This keeps the parts always moist and prevents friction. The membrane is called the *synovial membrane.* If it be cut or punctured, the joint-water runs out, and the joint is stiff until it heals up and is resupplied. A disease of the membrane may produce permanent stiffness of the joint.

6. Kinds of Joints. — There are many kinds of joints, some permitting much motion in all directions, others scarcely any motion at all. The most freely movable joints are in the limbs, where the greatest motion is needed. The hip joint is called a ball-and-socket joint, because the end of the femur is rounded, like a ball, and fits perfectly into a cup-like cavity or socket in the innominata bone. This permits motion in all directions. The shoulder joint is similar, but the cavity is not so deep, which permits still greater freedom of motion. The knee, ankle, and elbow are hinge joints, permitting motion in two directions only, back and forth.

—·◦·—

LESSON 7.

The Muscles.

1. What are Muscles ? — They are the lean meat, or flesh, of an animal. They give the general form to the body and make up the greater part of its weight. All the motions of the body are produced by the contractions of these bundles of fibers we call muscles. They are found

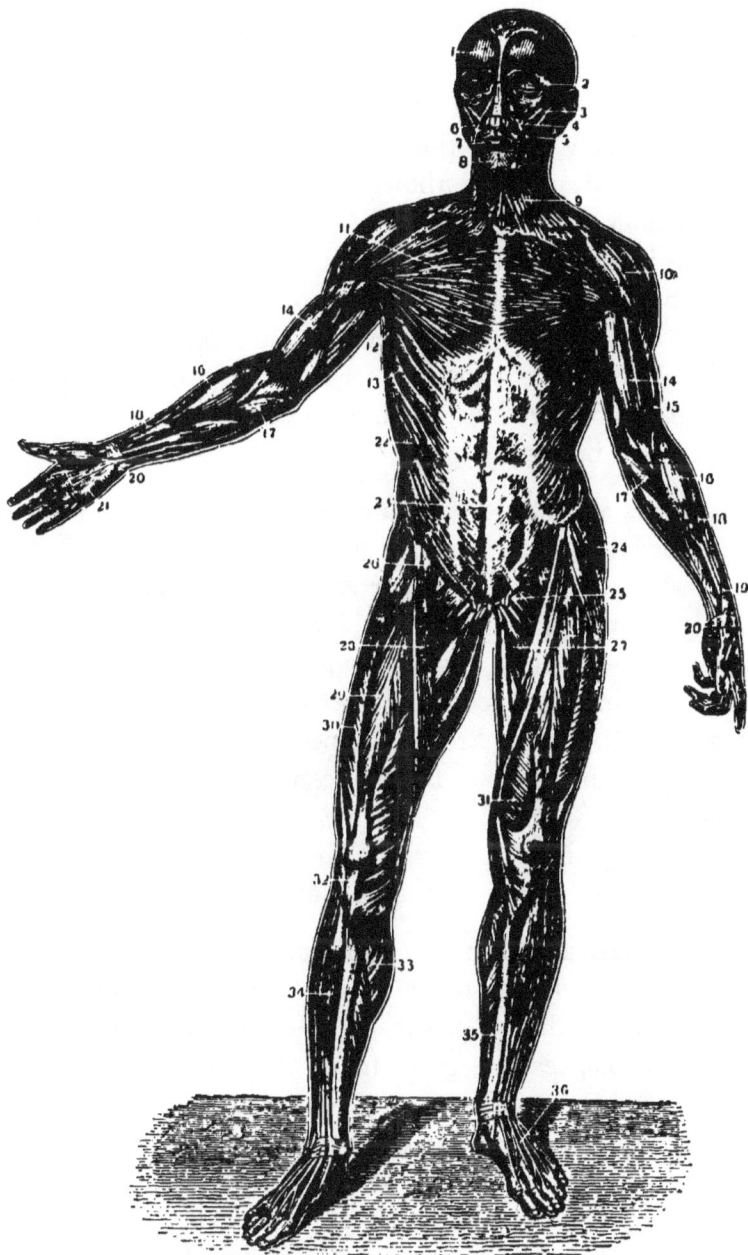

FIG. 6.

in the skin and cause it to draw up into little lumps when
our bodies are chilled, producing what is often called
"goose-flesh." They are found in the stomach and intestines, and their contraction causes the food to move along
during digestion. Swallowing is produced by muscles.
The various changes in the voice are caused by minute
muscles in the throat. We exercise a tiny muscle in the
ear when we listen to sounds, and one in the eye when we
look at near objects. The heart is one large muscle. The
bones are concealed nearly everywhere by muscles, which
in contracting produce all their motions. Thus, you see,
muscles are important parts of the body.

2. **Sizes and Shapes of Muscles.** — The longest muscle
in the body extends from the hip bone to the tibia, about
two feet in length. The shortest is in the middle ear and
is only a small fraction of an inch long. There are all
sizes between these two extremes. The most common
shape is spindle-shaped (thick in the middle and tapering
to each end). Some are fan-shaped, others like a feather,
the fibers running out from a central line. A few are
circular, and when they contract they diminish or close
the opening they surround. There is one such around
the mouth and another around the eye.

3. **Number and Names of Muscles.** — Most of the muscles are in pairs, one on each side of the body. There are
about five hundred distinct muscles in the body, having
special names, beside a great many sets of muscular fibers,
which have no special name. The names, like those of
the bones, are all in Latin or Greek and have each a
significance. Thus some are named from their shape
resembling some object, others from their location near or
upon some bone, others again from their action or use.

4. The Tendons, or Sinews. — As muscles are the movers of the body, they must in some way be fastened to bones and other parts. Sometimes they are attached directly to the bones, but usually by strong, fibrous cords or bands called *tendons*. In some cases the tendons are much longer than the muscles. When you close your fist tightly, you will observe cords standing out under the skin of the wrist. These are the tendons of the muscles which move the fingers. Muscles are in some cases attached to cartilages, to ligaments, to the skin, and to other muscles. The large tendon, which is attached to the heel bone, and which can be felt behind the ankle, is called the **Tendon of Achilles.** It was so named because, as the story goes, Achilles, the Greek warrior, was dipped by his mother in the river Styx, and thus made incapable of being injured. But she held him by the heel and this part did not get dipped, and it so happened that he was wounded in this part and died from the effects of the wound. This tendon is sometimes too short, and the heel is drawn up, causing the deformity known as " club-foot." It can frequently be cured by a surgical operation which consists of simply cutting the tendon beneath the skin, in which case the space fills up and the tendon becomes lengthened. Children with deformed limbs should be examined by competent surgeons, as in many cases they may be cured by simple operations.

5. Structure of Muscles. — Take a piece of boiled meat and examine it. You observe that it seems to be made up of fibers, or threads, lying side by side and in small bundles. You may strip off these fibers. Maybe you will get a dozen or more of them, appearing as one thread; but by careful picking you will finally split it up, until you have a thread finer than the finest hair, which you cannot further divide. This is called the ultimate fiber. The whole muscle is made up of these small threads, which seem to be held together by a fine, cobweb-like tissue. This tissue is called the **per-i-mys-i-um** (around muscle). It also forms a sheath, or coat, for the entire muscle.

6. Muscle Fibers under the Microscope. — If we place a single fiber under a microscope of high power, we see many dark lines running across the fiber and lengthwise, dividing it up into little blocks, or squares. These lines have been counted and there are as many as ten thousand in an inch. Each little block, or square, is supposed to be a *muscle cell*, yet this subject is not yet well understood. Muscles which have this appearance under the microscope are called *striped muscles;* and all such, except the heart, contract in obedience to the will and are said to be voluntary muscles. The muscles of the digestive organs and some others are purely involuntary and have a different appearance when magnified. They are made up of flat, tapering bands, interlaced in all directions, and are called *unstriped muscles.*

LESSON 8.

The Uses of Muscles.

1. How Muscles Act. —Muscles move the parts they are attached to by *contracting*, that is, they grow shorter and thicker, and thus pull upon the parts fastened to their ends. Muscles contract in obedience to the will, the power to make them contract being sent along a nerve, which is connected with the brain. But in an animal just killed they can be made to contract by touching the nerve which goes to them, by striking the muscles themselves, or by applying electricity or an acid to them. In frogs, snakes, and turtles, the muscles may be made to contract and the limbs to move hours after the animal is dead, in the turtle even after the lapse of four days or more. When a chicken's head is cut off with one blow of the axe, the irritation of the air upon the ends of the severed nerves causes its muscles to contract, and the animal jumps about in a lively manner, although it is dead and ceases to suffer the moment its head is cut off.

2. **The Instruments of Motion.** — As we have said, all motion in the body is produced by muscular contraction. There is one exception to this in the case of *cilia*, which will be described under the breathing organs. How important the power of motion is to an animal we can readily see. By contraction of muscles it is enabled to move from place to place and seek its food, also to seize its food and to carry itself away from danger. Even after the food is conveyed to the stomach, muscular action carries it to all parts of the body; for the food becomes a part of the blood, and muscular contraction of the heart and blood vessels sends the blood to every part.

3. **Language Depends on Muscular Action.** — The most universal language is that of signs and gestures made by the limbs. But all articulate language, or speech, is the result of muscular action. The human voice is capable of an almost infinite variety of sounds, and each is produced by variations in muscular contraction. The muscles of the face are capable of expressing a great variety of feeling, as of joy, sorrow, anger, fear, etc.

4. The Strength of Muscles. — A muscle is a soft, yielding mass easily torn apart ; yet, strange to say, a muscle contracting in obedience to the will can exert enormous force.   One man lifted 1442¼ pounds by his hands alone, and another, by means of harness attached to his body so that he could bring many muscles into action, lifted 3239 pounds.   We cannot understand this mysterious power, how such a weak thing can draw itself together and exert such enormous force.   It is an evidence of the wisdom and power of the Great Contriver of the Universe.   The work of the world, — the building of towns and cities, railroads and ships, the removal of the forests and the cultivation of the soil, the production of manufactured articles, the mining, the commerce, and even the education and moral improvement of mankind, — is, at the foundation, a result of muscular activity, guided and controlled by another force, mind activity.

5. The beauty of the human form depends largely upon muscular development.   It is true that the roundness and plumpness of form is due largely to the *fat* which fills out the spaces not occupied by muscles, yet the graceful tapering of limbs and the beauty of expression depend on the full development of muscles.

—◆—

LESSON 9.

The Care of Muscles.

1. Exercise. — If muscles are not exercised, they become weak and small.   Yet too much exercise is not good for them.   No muscle can work constantly.   It must have rest. The heart appears to be in constant motion, yet it is not. It contracts, and then there is a pause. If you were to add together the brief periods in which the muscle fibers of the heart are not acting, it would amount to as much as nine hours out of every twenty-four. A muscle may contract many times in succession without injury, but it cannot remain in a state of contraction very long without injury. To hold your arm out straight from the body requires the steady contraction of several muscles. Did you ever try to see how long you could hold it out? It very soon becomes painful. It is much easier to push it out and draw it back in rapid succession for several minutes than to keep it held out for the same length of time. When you push it out and draw it back, you allow one set of muscles to rest while the other set works. So in walking and in performing almost any kind of labor, muscles alternate with each other in resting and working.

2. **Rest.** — Rest is as important as exercise. The great secret of caring for our muscles consists in a proper alternation of exercise and rest for all the muscles in the body. This is not always easy to determine. When we have exercised a muscle too long, we feel tired. This is nature's warning that we must give the part a rest. But frequently our minds are engaged in thought, bent on accomplishing some work, and we do not regard the feeling of weariness, and thus overwork our muscles. Proper rest is not complete idleness. We may rest one part while another works. It requires one set of muscles to keep the body in a standing position and different muscles are brought into use in sitting; and even in standing and sitting in different positions different muscles are used. It is really easier to walk for an hour than to stand per-

fectly still for an hour, because in standing certain muscles must be kept in a state of contraction to keep the body upright, while in walking one set of muscles rest while another set is working. However, a slight shifting of position in standing will change the muscles and give them a partial rest.

3. **Avoid Violent Exercise.** — By rapid and powerful contraction muscles may be strained and injured. Running and leaping are not very likely to injure children, because their bodies are light and the muscular effort not very great ; yet in the effort to outrun or outleap a rival one may strain the muscles. Lifting heavy weights often results in strain of the muscles. *Long continued exercise, as in jumping a rope, may so excite the action of the heart as to cause its sudden paralysis, or it may result in the bursting of a blood vessel.* Such cases have occurred within the author's knowledge. Girls, in trying to see who could jump a rope the greatest number of times in succession, have suddenly dropped dead from failure of the heart or bursting of a blood vessel.

4. **Other Parts Benefited by Exercise.** — When the entire body is exercised, as in walking and running, the heart beats more rapidly and we breathe faster, and thus more blood is sent to every part of the body, and the impurities are more rapidly thrown off through the lungs. The perspiration is also increased, and thus impurities are thrown out. When not overdone, this is very beneficial to all parts, including the muscles themselves, as they receive more nourishment from a better circulation and purification of the blood. The power of digestion and the action of the liver and other glands are also increased by muscular exercise. The nervous system is also bene-

fited, and the mind made clearer by proper exercise of the muscular system. *You can always study better after a proper amount of exercise.*

5. **Kinds of Exercise to be Recommended.** — The person's occupation in some cases gives him the proper amount and variety of exercise. The farmer and many mechanics usually get enough exercise in their daily occupations. They need guard only against overwork and straining their muscles. But persons whose occupation requires a sitting posture, and those whose work is mental rather than physical, should take exercise which will bring into use those muscles that are not used in the ordinary work.

Walking is good exercise for nearly all people. It brings into use a large number of muscles. *Horseback riding* is largely a passive kind of exercise, benefiting organs by the gentle shaking it gives them. It is useful to persons who are not strong. *Carriage riding* gives but little exercise, but for invalids and very delicate persons it is good. *Out-door games* are valuable, but in some, as base-ball and foot-ball, there is danger of making the exercise too violent. *Gymnastic exercises*, such as swinging clubs, dumb-bells, climbing and pulling on ropes, poles, etc., are useful when out-door exercise cannot be taken. There should always be a careful gradation in these exercises, as they may easily be overdone.

6. **Best Time for Exercise.** — The morning is generally the best time for exercise. The body has been resting during the night and can endure the exercise better. Persons who find themselves troubled with sleeplessness are often benefited by gentle exercise just before retiring. Only the most gentle exercise should be taken immedi--

ately before and after meals. The stomach requires the energies of the body at that time.

Exercise should be of a kind pleasurable in itself. When we are not conscious that we are exercising, it does us the most good. To take a walk merely as a task to be performed will not benefit us as much as to go out to gather flowers, insects, or shells. Every one should take an interest in some subject that would require excursions to the fields and woods, or be interested in the use of tools as a pastime for leisure hours.

7. Effects of Alcohol on the Muscles. — It was once thought that alcohol increased a man's strength, and it was the custom to serve out whiskey or some other alcoholic drink to " harvest hands "; but this is a mistake. Alcohol only *apparently* increases strength. It stimulates us to use all the strength we have. It is like a whip to a horse, making him *exert* his strength but adding nothing to his power. A drunken man staggers, and his voice is thick and husky. Sometimes he sees double and imagines other persons are staggering. This is because the alcohol so affects his brain as to destroy its control over the muscles. He staggers, because he cannot make one leg move in harmony with the other. The muscles of his tongue do not act properly, and he cannot articulate correctly. He cannot control the muscles which fix the eyes together on one object, so he sees a separate image with each eye. The eyeballs roll, and the images he sees appear to be unsteady. *A long-continued use of alcoholic liquors tends to permanent paralysis or unsteadiness of the muscles. By impairing digestion the muscles do not receive proper nourishment and are thus in time weakened.*

8. Tobacco on the Muscles. — *Those who use tobacco to excess are frequently troubled with trembling or nervousness, caused by the effect of the tobacco on the muscles through the nervous system. Young persons are more apt to be injured than those in middle or old age.*

LESSON 10.

Bones and Muscles. — A Review.

[To TEACHER AND PUPIL. — Frequent reviews are important. If the pupil can answer in an intelligent manner the majority of the following questions, he certainly knows a good deal about bones and muscles. This lesson may be divided into two or three lessons if the teacher think proper.]

1. How does a bone differ from a piece of wood? From a stone?

2. What does a hot fire remove from a bone? How does a burned bone differ from one that is not burned? What does an acid remove from a bone? How does a bone which has been soaked in acid differ from one that has not?

3. What proportion of a bone is gelatine? What proportion is earthy matter? What qualities does the gelatine give to bone? What does the earthy matter give?

4. State the differences between young and old bones. Suppose the bones of a grown man were exactly like those of a child, what would be the result? Suppose the bones of a child were exactly like those of an old man, what would very likely happen?

5. Can you describe the appearance of a slice of bone under the microscope? What are Haversian canals? What are canaliculi? What are lacunæ?

6. What are bones in an early stage of their growth? The process of changing from their first condition to true bone is called *ossification*. When does ossification take place?

7. What covers bones? From what do they get their nourishment?

8. What is the skeleton? Why does a human body need a skeleton? What protects the delicate and soft parts of the body from injury?

9. How do bones aid in the movements of the body? Would muscles be of any use without bones?

10. Name some of the uses to which animal bones may be put. What is shoe-blacking made from?

11. How many bones in the body? How many are single? How many in the central line of the body? How many *pairs of bones* are there?

12. Write the names of as many bones of the head as you can call to mind. What bone forms the forehead? What ones are used in chewing the food? Where is the *vomer?* The *ethmoid?* The *temporal?*

13. How many bones in the head? In the face? In the trunk? In the upper limb? In the lower limb? In the arm? In the hand? In the wrist? In the ankle? In the foot?

14. What is a *vertebra?* What bones make the thorax? What the pelvis? Where is the sacrum?

15. What bone in the leg corresponds to the humerus of the arm?

16. How does alcohol affect the bones? Tight clothing? Why should you sit and stand erect?

17. What is the advantage of so many bones?

18. Describe ligaments. In a sprained ankle what part is injured?

19. What is the use of ligaments? Of cartilage in joints?

20. What is synovia? What is its use? Describe a ball-and-socket joint and give an example.

21. What are muscles? How many are there? What are tendons? What are they for? Why are they sometimes longer than the muscles?

22. How does a muscle fiber look under the microscope?

23. How do muscles act? What relation do muscles have to bones? Name some of the uses of muscles.

24. Why should we exercise? Why should we rest? Why is violent exercise unadvisable?

25. Why does the drunken man stagger? Why does he imagine others drunk? Why does he sometimes see double?

LESSON 11.

The Mouth and the Teeth.

1. **The Mouth.** — The mouth is for the reception of food, although in man it answers other purposes as well. It is the place where *articulate sounds* are made principally, by the help of the tongue, teeth, and lips. The tongue, when at rest, forms the principal part of the *floor* of the mouth. The *roof* of the mouth is formed by a part of the superior maxillary bone and part of the palate bone.

The back part of the mouth is called the *fau-ces*. It has an opening into a cavity called the *phar-ynx*. From the top of this opening hangs, like a little curtain, the *u-vu-la*, or hanging palate, and on either side are the *ton-sils*, two peculiar glands the uses of which are not known. They sometimes become inflamed, producing the disease known as *quinsy* or *ton-sil-i-tis*. The lips form the front of the mouth and the cheeks the sides. Each cheek is mainly made up of a muscle, which, when it contracts, keeps the food between the teeth. It is brought into use in blowing

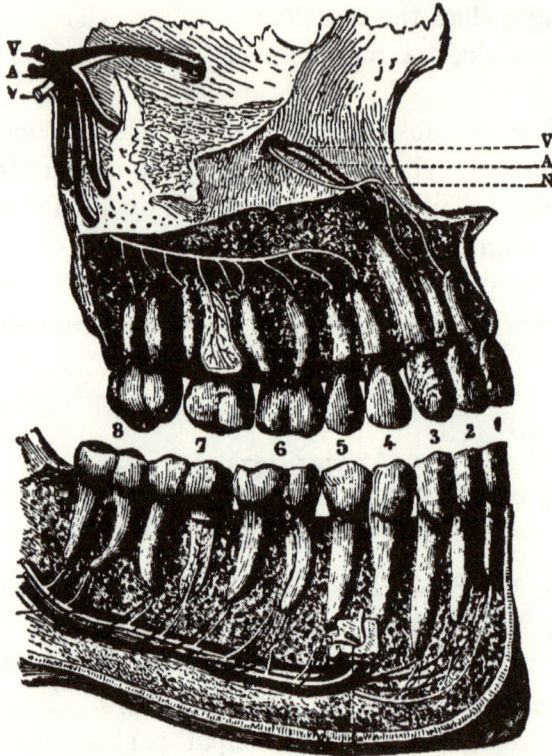

Fig. 7.

a trumpet, hence it is called the *buc-cin-a-tor*, or trumpeter. The entire inside of the mouth is lined with mucous membrane, which will be explained in another place, as it is only a part of the membrane that lines the whole of the digestive tube, or canal

2. **The Temporary Teeth.**—Usually, when a child is about seven months old, two teeth appear in the front part of the lower jaw, and shortly after two above them in the upper jaw. A few months later one appears on each side of the two central ones, above and below, making four more. At the end of the second or third year, sometimes later, there will be twenty teeth, ten in each jaw. At the age of six years, or later, these teeth begin to come out, and others grow up to take their places. These first teeth are called *temporary*, or *milk teeth*. The roots of the temporary teeth are absorbed; that is, the material which composes them is torn down gradually and carried away in the blood. This absorption is caused by the new teeth pressing against them from below. When the root is nearly all absorbed, the tooth becomes loose and falls out or is removed. It sometimes happens that the new teeth begin to grow out at the side of the old ones, and if the old ones are not pulled out crooked teeth will be the result.

3. **The Permanent Teeth.**—There are thirty-two of the second, or permanent, set of teeth, sixteen in each jaw. There are four kinds of teeth, each kind differing in shape and position and used for different purposes. The four front teeth in each jaw are called **in-ci-sors** (cutters). They are thin, broad, and sharp, somewhat like a chisel. They are for the purpose of cutting the food. On each side of each set of incisors is one **ca-nine** (dog) tooth, making four in all. They are pointed and a little longer than the other teeth. They help to seize and tear the food. In the dog and cat they are very long and sharp and are called "tushes." Behind each canine tooth are two **bi-cus-pids** (two-pointed), making eight in all. They have each two points and are partly for tearing and

partly for grinding and crushing the food. Back of the
bicuspids are the **mo-lars** (grinders), six in each jaw.
Those in the upper jaw have five points, and those in the
lower jaw four. They are larger and stronger than the
other teeth and are for the purpose of crushing and
grinding the food.

4. Parts of a Tooth.— Each tooth has a *crown*, or top
portion, a *root*, or *fang*, which is buried in the jaw bone,
and a *neck*, or slightly narrowed portion, between crown
and root, covered by the *gums*. The gums consist of a
fibrous material covered with mucous membrane. The
incisor, canine, and bicuspid teeth have each but one root.
The upper molars have three roots, the lower two.

5. The Structure of a Tooth. — Each tooth contains a
cavity, which during life is filled with a soft substance
called *dental pulp*. This contains nerves and blood vessels, and from it the tooth gets its nourishment. The
body of the tooth consists of white substance harder than
bone, called **den-tine.** The crown of the tooth is covered
with a very hard substance, the **en-am-el.** It is not only
the hardest substance in the human body, but the hardest
in the animal and vegetable kingdoms, and one of the
most durable. It is harder than iron and most of the
metals. The root of the tooth is covered with a substance
called *cement*, which is very similar to bone.

6. The Time and Order of Appearance of the Teeth.—
The time differs in different persons, but the order is
always the same. Usually the temporary teeth appear as
follows : —

7th month, two middle incisors.
9th month, two side incisors.

13th month, first, or front, molars.

18th month, canines.

One and a half to three years, last molars.

The permanent teeth appear: —

6½ years, first molars.

7th year, two middle incisors.

8th year, two side incisors.

9th year, first bicuspid.

10th year, second bicuspid.

11th to 12th year, canine.

12th to 13th year, second molars.

17th to 21st year, last molar.

The last molar is called the wisdom tooth. It is usually smaller than the other molars.

7. **Uses of the Teeth.**— You know that the teeth are for the purpose of dividing the food and preparing it for swallowing. In animals they serve to secure their food and for defence. In man they help to articulate sounds. Certain letters cannot be pronounced without the aid of the teeth. They also add to the beauty of the human face.

LESSON 12.

The Road to the Stomach.

1. **The Salivary Glands.** — The mouth is the beginning of a tube which is about thirty feet in length, called the alimentary (food) canal. Certain glands manufacture fluids from the blood and pour them into this canal at various places. These fluids are the principal agents in digesting the food. The first fluid which is poured into the alimentary canal is the **saliva.** This fluid is secreted,

or manufactured, in certain glands called *salivary glands*.
There are three pairs of them. The **pa-rot-id** is the largest. It lies beneath the skin just in front of the ear, and
pours its secretion into the back part of the mouth through
a tube called *Stenson's duct*. The next largest is the *sub-
maxillary*, just below the angle of the lower jaw. It has
a duct, or outlet, also. The *sublingual* is the other gland,
lying just beneath the tongue. It has a number of small
ducts. These glands consist of many little bags arranged
something like a bunch of grapes; each tiny bag has a
tube, which unites with others; and finally all empty into
the duct of the gland. *The saliva changes starch to sugar.*

2. **The Pharynx.** — We have said that in the back part
of the mouth was an opening into the pharynx. This
is a short, wide tube, composed of muscles and lined with
mucous membrane. It has seven openings : one to the
mouth above; one to the gullet, or **e-soph-a-gus**, below;
one to the *larynx*, or beginning of the windpipe ; two to
the cavities of the nose; and two to the **Eu-sta-chi-an**
tubes, which lead to the middle ear. The pharynx receives the food from the mouth and passes it into the
esophagus.

3. **The Esophagus.** — This is the tube through which
the food passes into the stomach. It is about nine inches
long and lies behind the windpipe, the heart, and the
lungs. It is composed of muscular fibers lined with
mucous membrane. The muscular fibers of the outer
layer run lengthwise, and those of the inner layer run
circularly. The walls are soft and elastic and lie close
together except when food is passing. When a portion
of food enters the esophagus, a ring of muscular fibers contracts behind it, pushing it along a little way; and this is

followed by the contraction of another ring, and so on, until the food is forced into the stomach. A person can swallow when standing on his head just as well as in the natural upright position, as the muscles will force the food along. Children sometimes get hold of acids or alkalies, or other strong and poisonous substances, and drink them. If the result is not death, it may be a destruction of part of the mucous membrane of the mouth, pharynx, and esophagus; and when healing takes place, the esophagus (because its walls lie in contact with each other) grows partly or completely shut, so that little or no food can be swallowed. Turn to the lesson on Digestion, and see what is there said about the nourishing of the person in such a case.

4. **Remember** that the food is taken into the mouth, chewed, or **masticated**, by the **teeth**, aided by the *tongue* and *cheeks*, which help to keep it between the teeth, and by the **saliva**, which moistens it; then it passes into the **pharynx**, and we have no longer control of it, and from there to the **esophagus**, which carries it into the stomach, where it falls in little rounded masses called *boluses*. Here it undergoes further preparation.

LESSON 13.

The Stomach.

1. **Location.**— This important organ of digestion lies in the upper and mainly in the left part of the cavity of the abdomen. It must be remembered that the space between the neck and the hips is divided into two large cavities by a muscular partition called the **diaphragm**.

The cavity above the diaphragm is called the *thoracic cavity* and contains the heart and lungs; and the space below is called the *abdomen*, or abdominal cavity, and contains the stomach, intestines, liver, spleen, and kidneys. The stomach is an enlargement of the alimentary canal and a continuation of the esophagus.

2. Size and Shape. — The stomach is about twelve inches long, four inches broad, and two inches thick, and holds about three pints when moderately full. It is somewhat in the shape of a pear, larger at the upper, or left, end. The place where the esophagus ends and the stomach begins is called the *car-di-ac* orifice; and at the opposite end, where the intestine begins, is the *py-lo-ric* orifice. A fold of the mucous lining of the stomach forms a kind of valve or door. This is called the *py-lo-rus* (gate-keeper).

3. Structure. — The walls of the stomach are made up of four layers or coats. The inner is a mucous membrane, continuous with the lining of the esophagus and intestines. Next to this is a layer of loose tissue called the cellular coat, and next to this is the muscular coat. This consists of fibers, some of which run lengthwise, some circularly, and some diagonally. The outer coat is called a serous membrane, being a part of the membrane which lines the abdominal cavity and covers all organs within it. The mucous membrane contains many folds, or wrinkles, and cavities, which greatly increases the surface. Amidst these folds are numerous little glands which secrete the *gastric juice.*

4. Gastric Juice. — The gastric (stomach) juice is a clear, watery liquid, one of the principal agents in dissolving and preparing the food. It contains a peculiar substance called **pep-sin**, which has the power of changing *albuminous substances* (that is, substances resembling the white of an egg in chemical nature) into *albuminose,* in which condition they are fit to be absorbed and become a part of the blood. *Gastric juice has no effect on starch and sugar, nor on fats and oils.* These are changed by other fluids of digestion.

LESSON 14.

The Intestines.

1. The Small Intestine. — We have seen that the alimentary canal is first a cavity, the *mouth;* then a short, wide tube, the *pharynx;* then a long, narrow, straight tube, the *esophagus;* then a large bag, the *stomach.* Now it narrows down again to a tube about twenty feet long, coiled up in a mass in the center of the abdomen. This is divided, for convenience of study, into three parts, the **du-o-de-num**, the **je-ju-num**, and the **il-e-um**.

2. The Duodenum. — This is the part of the small intestine next to the stomach and is so called from the Latin word for twelve, as it is about as long as the width of twelve fingers, or about ten inches. It is very crooked, extending first upward from its connection with the stomach, then backward and to the right, then to the left, where it takes the name of *jejunum.*

3. The Jejunum. — This part of the small intestine was so named from the fact that it is always found empty after death, from a Latin word meaning "empty." It is about seven feet in length and is a little narrower than the duodenum.

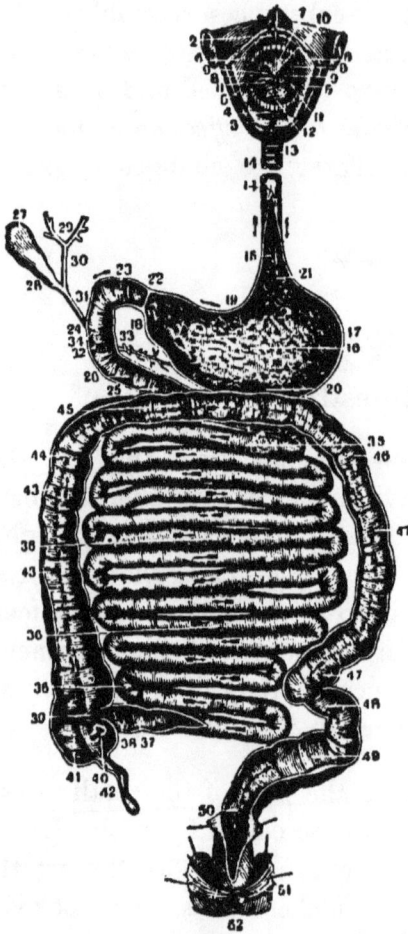

FIG. 8.

4. The Ileum. — The remaining part of the small intestine is called the ileum, from a word meaning " to twist," because it lies in many folds and coils.

5. Structure of the Small Intestine. — The walls of the small intestine are similar to that of the stomach, there being four coats: the inner, *mucous;* next, *muscular;* next, *cellular;* and outer, *serous.* The mucous and cellular coats are wrinkled by numerous folds, and these folds are covered with very tiny little projections as thick as the fibers of a piece of velvet. These little projections are called **vil-li** (singular, *villus,* meaning a tuft of hair). By this arrangement of folds and villi an enormous amount of surface is gained, a point of great importance in *absorption,* which will be explained in another lesson. Small glands are in the mucous coat. They secrete the *intestinal juice.*

6. **The Large Intestine.** — This portion of the alimentary canal does not appear like a simple enlargement of a tube, but like a wide tube closed at one end; and the small intestine, like a smaller tube, entering it at a point a little way from the closed end. The parts of the large intestine are the **coe-cum**, the **co-lon**, and the **rec-tum**.

7. **The Coecum.** — This is the closed end of the large intestine, or that part which projects beyond the place where the small intestine enters. It is so called because closed at one end, the word *coecum* meaning " blind." At its closed end is a small tube about as thick as a goose quill, called the *ver-mi-form* (worm-like) *appendix*. One should never swallow cherry stones and other hard seeds of fruits, as they have been known to lodge in this little tube and cause serious disease and even death.

8. **The Colon and Rectum.** — As you see in the picture, the colon lies around the small intestine, having an *ascending*, a *transverse*, and a *descending* portion, and ending, by a peculiar crook, in a straight tube, the *rectum*.

9. **Structure of Large Intestine.** — There is very little difference in the walls of the large and those of the small intestines. The large intestine has many folds, but no villi.

———

LESSON 15.

The Alimentary Canal. — A Review. .

1. What is the use of the mouth ? What forms the floor of the mouth ? The roof ? The sides ? What is the back part of the mouth called ? What is the uvula ? What are the tonsils ?

2. How many temporary teeth are there? Where do they first appear? What makes them come out?

3. How many permanent teeth? Describe the incisors; the canine teeth. What teeth stand behind the canines? Describe the molars. Name the uses of each of the kinds of teeth.

4. What are the parts of a tooth? What are the gums? What is found in the cavity of a living tooth?

5. What is enamel? Dentine? What is the hardest substance in the organic world? Can you cut the enamel of your teeth with a knife? No; but you may break a piece of it off by striking it with a piece of metal. Do not use a metal toothpick, or crack nuts with your teeth.

6. State the order in which the different kinds of temporary teeth appear. When do they begin to appear? When has a child a full set of temporary teeth?

7. When does the first permanent tooth appear? What happens to the temporary tooth that is in its way? What is the wisdom tooth?

8. State three uses of teeth. What is the alimentary canal? Its length? Name and locate the three pairs of salivary glands.

9. What is the use of the salivary glands? You will learn more about saliva in the lesson on Digestion.

10. Describe the pharynx. Name its openings. What is the use of the esophagus? How is the food carried into the stomach? A stone, if unsupported, *falls* toward the earth, we say, by the force of gravity. Does the force of gravity have anything to do with swallowing?

11. What part of the preparation of the food takes place in the mouth? What then receives the food? What next? What next?

12. Locate the stomach. What relation has it in loca-

tion to the heart and lungs? What organs lie below the diaphragm? What above?

13. State the size and shape and name the orifices of the stomach. What is the pylorus?

14. Name the coats of the stomach in proper order. How is the surface of the interior of the stomach increased?

15. What does the stomach secrete? What is the name of the peculiar fluid which helps digest (prepare) the food in the stomach? Does it affect starch? What fluid *does* act on starch?

16. What is the widest portion of the tube called the alimentary canal? What is the duodenum? The jejunum? The ileum? What is the length of the small intestine? Of the large intestine?

17. State the resemblances and differences between the large and small intestines, — in length, in thickness, and in structure. Name the parts of the large intestine.

18. What are villi? What is a villus? What is the vermiform appendix?

LESSON 16.

The Liver, Pancreas, and Spleen.

1. **What are Glands?** — Glands are organs which either separate materials from the blood or actually manufacture certain fluids by combining certain elements existing in the blood. These fluids usually serve important purposes in the body. Some glands are mere depressions in the mucous membrane, as the glands which secrete the mucus; others are complicated arrangements of cells and tubes, as the liver.

2. **The Location, Size, etc., of the Liver.** — You have all seen the liver, or a part of the liver, of an ox or pig. The human liver resembles the liver of these animals in general appearance. It is located in the right and upper portion of the abdominal cavity, just beneath the diaphragm. Its length from side to side is ten or twelve inches, its breadth from before backward is six or seven inches, and its thickness from above downward is about three inches. In a grown person it weighs three or four pounds.

3. **Structure of the Liver.** — To the naked eye the liver appears, when cut through, as a reddish brown mass, with tubes scattered here and there through it. Careful examination by the aid of the microscope shows that the liver is made up of minute rounded cells, held together by fibrous tissue, and intermingled with a dense network of tubes. These tubes are the branches of the various vessels of the liver, which are as follows: (1) The **por-tal vein**, which is made up of branches coming from the stomach, intestines, and spleen. It penetrates the liver and divides again and again, until it reaches by fine tubes every part. (2) The **he-pat-ic artery**, which supplies the liver with blood just as every other organ is supplied. (3) The **hepatic veins**, of which there are several, carry the blood *out of* the liver which has been carried *into* it by the hepatic artery and portal vein. (4) The hepatic duct, which begins among the cells of the liver as a network, and finally unites into one tube. This duct conveys the **bile** which is secreted by the liver, to the intestine. (5) The **lymphatics**, which form a part of a system which spreads through the body. They will be explained in another lesson.

4. **The Bile.** — This is one of the important fluids of the digestive system. It is a clear, yellowish, or greenish yellow, watery fluid. It is manufactured in the cells of the liver, passes into the fine branches of the hepatic duct and finally into the small intestine through the *common bile duct.* This duct is made by the joining of the hepatic duct and the *cystic duct,* which comes from the **bile cyst,** or *gall-bladder.* This is a bag which lies on the under side of the liver, and is for the purpose of containing the bile when digestion is not going on. Thus, while food is being digested in the intestine, the bile is gradually passing down from the liver into the intestine; but when there is no food to be digested in the intestine, the common bile duct closes. But the secretion goes on all the time in the liver, and there must be some place for the bile to be deposited. This place is the *gall-bladder.* The bile then backs up through the cystic duct and fills the gall-bladder, to pass down again when required in the intestine. This arrangement is something like a mill-pond, which accumulates a supply, or "head," of water while the mill is not running, to be used when the mill is running.

5. **The Uses of the Liver.** — The liver secretes, or manufactures, bile; but this is but one of its uses. It has other and more important uses. It has the peculiar power of storing up heat-making material. The heat-making food is mostly sugar, either taken as sugar itself or in the form of starch, which is converted into sugar by the saliva and pancreatic fluid. This sugar all passes into the liver with the blood and is there converted into an insoluble form, called **gly-co-gen** (a word meaning "sugar producer," so called because it is readily converted back to sugar).

Starch cannot be absorbed and taken into the blood. It is, therefore, converted into sugar in the alimentary canal and absorbed into the blood. Sugar cannot be stored up, as it dissolves so readily. It is, therefore, converted into glycogen for the purpose of storage, and this glycogen is converted back to sugar as the body demands it. If it were not for this wise arrangement, shortly after digestion the blood would have more heat-making material than could be used, and during the period of fasting there would not be enough. The liver, then, acts as a bank, receiving deposits in large sums and paying them out in small sums, as demanded.

6. **The Pancreas.** — This gland is called the "sweetbread" in animals. The word *pancreas* means "all flesh," so named from its appearance. It lies behind the stomach, and is somewhat like a dog's tongue in shape. It is six or eight inches long, one and a half inches broad, and from one-half to an inch thick, and weighs about three ounces. In structure it is very similar to the salivary glands. It secretes a fluid, which, like the saliva, converts starch into sugar and, like the gastric juice, converts albuminous foods into *albuminose*, and also acts upon the fats, changing them into a form capable of being absorbed. The fluid passes out by a duct into the duodenum.

7. **The Spleen.** — As very little is known of the use of this organ, we need say but little about it. It is an oblong, dark-colored body, somewhat in appearance like the liver, and weighs usually about seven ounces; but in certain diseases it has been known to increase to twenty pounds in weight. It secretes no fluid, but numerous blood vessels pass into it and through it and out again. It is supposed to effect some changes in the blood and to

act as a reservoir for the increased amount of blood produced during digestion.

LESSON 17.

Digestion.

1. **What is Digestion?** — We have used this word several times already in this book, and you, perhaps, have
some idea of its meaning. You will say that it is the
process of preparing the food to be used by the body.
The word *digest* means literally " to cook," but digestion
is a different kind of preparation. The preparation is
such a change on the food as will render it capable of
being absorbed ; that is, taken into the blood vessels which
circulate it through the body. Some portions of some
kinds of food are not digested at all. The grape sugar
which is found in fruits is simply absorbed, also the water,
which may be considered a part of the food. Other substances, however, could not pass into the blood vessels
and must undergo a chemical change. Digestion also
includes the mechanical division of the food ; that is, the
crushing, grinding, breaking, or dissolving action necessary
to reduce it to a fine state, so that the fluids of digestion
may act upon it.

2. **Steps in the Process of Digestion.** — The food is
first taken into the mouth and there chewed, or masticated,
and at the same time thoroughly mixed with the saliva.
The next step is swallowing, which is simply the process
of passing from the mouth to the pharynx and through
the esophagus to the stomach.

In the stomach the food is thoroughly mixed with the gastric juice and is reduced to a half-fluid state called **chyme.** This mixing and dissolving action is aided by a peculiar churning motion of the stomach, caused by contractions of the muscular fibers in its walls. By this action the food is made to pass round and round in the stomach from one end to the other and back again, the *pylorus*, or valve at the lower end, preventing the contents from escaping into the duodenum until it is thoroughly dissolved. If there is any solid substance which cannot be dissolved by the stomach, it is apt to work its way through the pyloric valve and escape into the duodenum before digestion is completed. The saliva does not act in the stomach, because it is chemically of an opposite nature to the gastric juice and cannot act in its presence. But its action is resumed in the intestine, where the gastric juice is neutralized by the fluids found there.

The chyme passes into the small intestine and is acted upon by the bile, the pancreatic juice, and the intestinal juice. These fluids complete the process of digestion. The part of the chyme which can be absorbed and used as nourishment is, after it has been acted upon by the intestinal fluids, called **chyle.** The portions which are indigestible pass on in the intestine as waste material.

To sum up, then, the steps in the process of digestion proper are: (1) *chewing,* (2) *swallowing,* (3) *stomach preparation,* or *chymification,* (4) *intestinal preparation,* or *chylification.*

3. **What is Chyle?**— It is a milky, white fluid containing all the nourishing part of the food except a part of certain portions, mostly sugar, which has been absorbed by the veins of the stomach. Its white appearance is

caused by the fat of the food, which is broken up into very minute globules.

4. What is Absorption?— Though not a part of the process of digestion proper, it is intimately connected with it and should be thoroughly understood before proceeding further. It is the process of sucking in, or taking up of, the nourishing part of the food from the alimentary canal, by the blood vessels. Absorption is accomplished in two ways, by the veins of the mucous membrane of the alimentary canal and by certain organs called **lac-te-als.** These are fine thread-like tubes, which begin in the villi of the small intestine and unite with larger and larger ones until they finally empty into a large tube called the **thoracic duct.** This lies along the spinal column, back of the stomach and intestines, and is connected with one of the large veins of the body, into which its contents empty. The lacteals are for the special purpose of absorbing fats, which cannot be absorbed directly by the blood vessels. They absorb other substances also. The nourishing parts of the food, or, in other words, the digested food, then, gets into the blood either directly by absorption through the veins, or indirectly by first passing through the lacteals and thoracic duct and then into the veins.

During the short time the food is in the mouth, pharynx, and esophagus there can be but little chemical change and but little absorption, yet there is some of both. If certain poisons be taken in the mouth, they may be immediately absorbed and produce death without a particle even reaching the stomach. Thirst may be quenched by merely holding water in the mouth, and the effect of medicine may be obtained in a similar manner.

Plants and some of the lowest forms of animal life do

not digest food, but simply absorb the material which surrounds them, selecting that which is adapted to their nourishment.

———◆◆◆———

LESSON 18.

Food and Drink.

1. **What is Food?** — This looks like a very easy question to answer, yet it is not so easy to give a correct
answer.   Food is whatever can be used in building up the
tissues of the body or in furnishing by its combustion a
supply of animal heat.   This gives rise to another question.   What is animal heat?

2. **Animal Heat.** — It is a peculiar fact that, no matter
how cold or hot the temperature of the atmosphere sur-
rounding us may be so long as life lasts (except in some
cases of disease), the temperature of the blood remains
very nearly the same, that is, about ninety-eight degrees
Fahrenheit.   A man may go into an oven heated to three
hundred and fifty degrees, and again endure for a time a
temperature of forty degrees below zero, and yet the temperature of his blood will be but slightly changed.   The
reason of this is that in the second case more heat is produced by the combustion of material in the body as fast
as it is conducted away by the atmosphere, and in the
first case the perspiration by its rapid evaporation cools
the body.   Animal heat is heat produced by the combustion of fuel in the body, the fuel being partly the food
and partly the tissues of the body, which are consumed to
make room for new tissues, that are constantly being produced.

3. **Assimilation.** — This word means "making like or similar to." It is applied to the process of building up the tissues from the material furnished by the blood. The blood gets its new material from the food. The cells of the body are constantly changing. Old ones disappear, and the material of which they are composed passes out of the body and is called waste material. The new cells which take their place are made from the new material in the blood. New material (food) is also needed for the increase in size of the body. It is said that in seven years all the substance of the body has been removed and new material taken its place. This is a mere guess, as we do not know how long it takes; but we do know that old cells are removed and new cells take their places. The rate at which this change goes on varies in different tissues. The cells of the mucous membrane of the stomach are said to be renewed several times during the act of digestion. The bones and other hard tissues are renewed more slowly, the enamel of the teeth, perhaps, not more than once or twice in a lifetime.

4. **Food Classified.** — All those foods which tend to produce heat in the body we shall call **heat-making** foods, and those which supply the waste and build up the tissues we shall call **tissue-making** foods. The heat-making foods are mainly those which contain carbon. They are **sugar, starch,** and **fats.** Oil is only a fat which remains liquid at ordinary temperature. The tissue-making foods are mainly those that contain nitrogen as well as carbon. They are often called for this reason *nitrogenous foods;* and, as they resemble albumen (a substance nearly pure in the white of an egg), they are sometimes called *albuminous foods.* Sugar, starch, and fat are also frequently

spoken of as *carbonaceous foods*. Sugar is found in most fruits, a small amount in grains and in garden vegetables; but the principal supply is from the juice of the sugar cane and from the beet root. Starch is abundant in potatoes and all grains. Our supply of fats comes from the flesh of animals, from butter, and a small amount from grains and nuts. Albuminous foods exist in the form of *albumen* proper in eggs, *fibrin* in lean meat, *gelatine* in bones and fibrous tissue, *gluten* in wheat, *legumin* in peas and beans, and *casein* in milk. Eggs and milk are perfect foods, as they contain a proper proportion of heat-making and tissue-making elements.

5. **Proper Selection of Food.** — In winter and in cold countries our bodies lose heat rapidly and we need to eat more of the heat-making food, that is, substances containing sugar, starch, and fat; in summer and in warm countries, a greater proportion of tissue-making food. The temperature of the body is nearly always a little higher than the atmosphere, even in the warmest countries; therefore the supply of heat-making food should at all times be greater.

6. **Water.** — All drinks that can be taken in any except very small quantities must be composed ·in the greater part of water. Tea, coffee, and chocolate, the common table drinks, are almost entirely water. Water is necessary: (1) to soften and dissolve the food so that it can be masticated and swallowed. (The saliva is mostly water and hence it aids in masticating and swallowing. All food contains at least some water); (2) to keep substances in solution while moving in the body; (3) to carry the waste material out of the body; (4) to cool the body by evaporation of the perspiration.

LESSON 19.

The Care of the Digestive Organs.

1. It is very important that we know how to care for the organs that are engaged in the great work of preparing the material which keeps our bodies in working condition; for it is not what we eat, but what we digest and assimilate, that makes us strong and keeps us alive. We may eat too much or not enough; our food may be unwholesome or improperly selected. The digestive organs may be injured in many ways and rendered unable to perform their proper work.

2. **Quantity of Food.** — The *appetite*, if not perverted, is a very good guide as to the proper quantity of food to eat. The appetite is natural so long as the food is plain and we take sufficient exercise and avoid exposures and other causes of ill health. *Indulgence in food simply to gratify the taste for certain articles will soon pervert the appetite.* One should eat from a natural desire for food and not simply because a certain article pleases our sense of taste. It is true our food should taste good to us, but it must be remembered that the plainest and simplest articles of diet will taste good if we have a real appetite.

The quantity of food necessary depends on a number of conditions. (1) A little more is required by persons during their *growing period*, in proportion to their size, than after the period of growth is completed. (2) In cold climates and in winter a little more food is needed than in warm climates and in summer. (3) Persons who labor need more than those who do not.

3. **Quality of Food.** — (1) Food should be *wholesome*, that is, free from any poisonous elements. Meats which

are "tainted" frequently contain poisonous substances produced in the decay of the flesh. Stale and partly decayed vegetables are also unwholesome for the same reason. Food from plants and animals affected with disease is usually unwholesome. (2) Food should not be too highly concentrated. A certain amount of bulk is necessary, as the stomach acts better on a large than on a small quantity; and a certain amount of mere waste matter stimulates the stomach and intestines and increases their action. (3) Food should not be too easy of digestion, as then the stomach does not have sufficient exercise; nor too difficult, as then it is overworked. (4) Food should contain a proper portion of heat-making and tissue-making elements. In winter we should eat starchy and sweet foods and more fat; in summer, more acid fruits and lean meats and soups. (5) A proper mixture of animal and vegetable food is, perhaps, the best, although there are some who think a purely vegetable diet is to be preferred.

4. **Cooking.** — Cooking renders many kinds of food more easy of digestion by softening it and making it more soluble. It also improves the flavor. Many kinds of meat, especially pork, are apt to contain the germs of certain parasites, or worm-like animals, which, if taken into the stomach, grow and multiply and produce sometimes fatal disease. Heating meat to the boiling point destroys these germs and renders it safe. *Never eat raw meat of any kind.* Frying meats, as ordinarily practiced, renders them indigestible. If the fat be very hot when the meat is put in, it does not penetrate the meat and does not injure it.

Warm food is usually better than cold food, as it corresponds more nearly with the natural temperature of the stomach.

5. **Variety of Food.** — The system seems to demand a variety of food. The same kind of food, however nutritious, when prepared exactly the same way soon becomes unpalatable.

6. **Regularity in Eating.** — The stomach tends to act periodically, that is, at regular recurring periods it is in better condition for digesting food. Meals at regular intervals of time seem to be better than when not regular, as the sensation of hunger will recur at about the same time, and if not gratified at the time it passes away, and then, if we eat, we lose much of the proper enjoyment of the food. The appetite is not then a good guide, and we may eat too much or too little.

7. **Eating between Meals.** — This is a bad practice. The stomach needs rest, and when food is taken too often it is constantly in exercise. *Persons who are continually eating nuts, candy, or fruit between meals are very apt to have dyspepsia in time.*

8. **Take Plenty of Time to Eat.** — One should eat slowly, taking time to masticate the food thoroughly. This gives the salivary and gastric glands also time to secrete the proper amount of fluid. Lively conversation and humor at the table favors digestion and prevents eating too rapidly.

9. **Warm and Cold Drinks.** — Warm drinks are generally favorable to the action of the stomach. *Ice-cold drinks lower the temperature of the stomach too much and ought not to be indulged in to any great extent.*

10. The Use of Condiments. — Condiments are such substances as salt, spices, and vinegar, which are not foods, but frequently render foods more palatable. If indulged in to any great extent, they are apt to inflame the coats of the stomach and produce dyspepsia. *Children especially should not eat their food highly seasoned.*

11. Fluids at Meals. — It is frequently stated that much fluid taken with the food retards digestion by diluting the gastric juice, but there is no good reason for supposing them injurious. One should use proper judgment, of course, as an excessive quantity would be injurious. It is an almost universal custom to drink something at meals.

12. The Use of Tea, Coffee, and Chocolate. — These drinks have but little effect directly on the digestive organs, but when used in excessive quantities they produce an injurious effect on the nervous system, especially in some persons, and thus they indirectly affect digestion. Young persons do not need such drinks, and they are frequently injurious during the growing period of life. *Milk and water should be the only drinks for young people.*

13. Tobacco. — The use of tobacco, either by smoking or chewing, frequently causes dyspepsia of the worst form. In chewing tobacco the salivary glands are unduly excited, and the saliva thus produced is thrown away. The result is a weakening of the glands. Acting through the nervous system, tobacco frequently produces very injurious effects on the organs of circulation and digestion. *Physicians all agree that tobacco is very injurious to the young.*

14. Alcohol and Digestion. — Alcohol is not a food, but a poison, in the true sense of that word. Small quantities well diluted, as in weak wines and in beer and ale, may for a time stimulate a weak stomach and thus improve digestion; but in time the organs are weakened, and more harm than good is done even by the mildest liquors. The liver is especially affected by a habitual use of alcoholic liquors. The livers of drunkards are often found covered with hard lumps, and sometimes there is a change of a part of the substance of the liver into fat. Like tobacco, alcohol is much more injurious to young persons than to adults. *If a habit of using either liquor or tobacco be formed while young, it is next to impossible to break off when older, and the habit is apt to grow until excessive quantities are used. The first cigar and the first glass of liquor are the ruin of many a promising young man.*

15. **Care of the Teeth.** — The teeth are, perhaps, the least important of the digestive organs, and it is a peculiar fact that no matter how well they be cared for they will sometimes begin to decay at an early age. But in many cases the early decay is due to neglecting to keep them clean. Use a soft tooth brush after each meal with a little very mild soap and water. *Do not use a metal toothpick, as it is apt to chip off the enamel. Do not bite threads or crack nuts with the teeth. Very hot and very cold drinks tend to crack the enamel. If you would have a sweet breath, keep the teeth clean.*

LESSON 20.

Review of the Digestive System.

1. Define a gland. What is the largest gland in the body ? The liver. Locate the liver. Name the vessels

of the liver.   What vessels carry material *into* the liver?
The portal vein and the hepatic artery.   What vessels
carry material out of the liver?   The hepatic veins, the
hepatic duct, and the lymphatics.

2. What is bile?   How does the bile get into the
intestine?   How does it get into the gall-bladder?

3. Name two uses of the liver.   What relation has the
liver to the sugar which is absorbed in the stomach?
Why is the liver like a bank?

4. Locate the pancreas.   What is the use of this gland?
What is the effect of the pancreatic fluid on food?   In
what respect is the pancreatic juice like saliva?

5. Tell all you know about the spleen.   (It has been
taken out of animals without any noticeable effect following its removal.)

6. Define digestion.   What part of the digestive process is performed in the mouth?   In the stomach?   In
the small intestine?   What is the use of the "pylorus"?

7. What is chyme?   Chyle?   What is the color of
chyle?

8. Explain absorption.   What kind of substances can
be absorbed?   Only those that are in a state of solution,
or, in other words, in a liquid form.   What are the
lacteals?   What is the thoracic duct?   What does it
carry?   Into what does it empty?

9. Define food.   What are the two uses of food?   What
produces the heat of the body?

10. What is meant by assimilation?   Is it correct to
say that what is a part of an apple, an egg, or a head of
cabbage to-day, may be a part of your bones, muscles, and
nerves to-morrow?

11. State whether each of the following-named substances is a heat-making or tissue-making food.   Sugar,

albumen, fibrin, starch, oil, casein, legumin. Suppose
you make a meal of bread and butter, do you get heat-
making material? Yes, from the oil of the butter and
from the starch and sugar of the bread. Do you get any
tissue-making material? Yes, from the gluten of the
bread.

12. Name three articles of food better suited for cold
weather. What is the use of water in the system?

13. Should the mere taste of the food guide us in
determining the quantity we should eat? Why should
a laboring man eat more than one who does not labor?

14. What is the objection to eating tainted meat and
stale or decayed vegetables?

15. Why do we cook food? What danger in eating
raw meat? Why is warm food better than cold?

16. Why should meals be regular? What is the
objection to eating between meals? Why should one
eat slowly?

17. What can be said about warm and cold drinks?
The use of spices, salt, and vinegar?

18. What of the effects of tea, coffee, and chocolate,
on the digestive organs? Of tobacco? Of alcohol? Is
alcohol a food?

19. How care for the teeth?

LESSON 21.

The Heart.

1. **Definition.** — We have learned that the blood is manufactured by the digestive organs from the food. Some
means for its perfect circulation through the body is

necessary. The heart and blood vessels are the means. The heart is a muscular pump, which by its contractions forces the blood into one set of vessels called arteries and draws it from another set called veins, thus producing a constant flow from a central point to the remotest parts of the body and back again.

2. **Location.** — The heart lies between the lungs, the greater portion being a little to the left of the middle of the chest. The larger end points upward, backward, and toward the right; the smaller end, downward, forward, and toward the left. The smaller end can be felt, when it beats, at a point between the cartilage of the fifth and sixth ribs, a little to the left of the sternum.

3. **Size and Shape.** — The human heart is about three and one half inches long, two and one half inches thick, and weighs from eight to twelve ounces in a grown person; or it is very near the size of the person's fist. The heart of a hog or sheep when full-grown is very nearly the same size and shape of a human heart.

4. **Cavities.** — The heart is a double organ, a partition running through it lengthwise dividing it into right and left sides. The right side pumps impure blood from the body to the lungs, and the left side pumps pure blood received from the lungs to all parts of the body. Each side has two cavities, the upper ones called **auricles**, which receive the blood, and the lower called **ventricles**, which discharge the blood.

5. **The Right Auricle.** — This cavity is a little larger than the left auricle and has thinner walls. It receives the blood from the entire body through two main tubes, the *superior vena cava*, which brings it from the upper

part of the body, and the *inferior vena cava*, which brings it from the lower part of the body and discharges the blood through an opening into the right ventricle. The blood which circulates through the walls of the heart itself is also returned to the right auricle through one large vein (the *coronary vein*) and a number of very small ones.

6. The Right Ventricle. — This cavity is the same size as the left ventricle, but has much thinner walls. The blood is prevented from returning to the right auricle by three triangular flaps of membrane, hanging from the opening and connected by fibrous cords to fleshy columns on the sides of the cavity of the ventricle. The blood can pass through these flaps, but when the ventricle contracts it cannot go back, as the blood gets behind them and they are pushed together. This arrangement is called the **tri-cus-pid** (three-pointed) **valve.** When the ventricle contracts, the blood is forced into the pulmonary artery and through it to the lungs. It is prevented from returning by three pockets of membrane, which open toward the artery. When the blood passes from the ventricle, they offer no hindrance; but it is prevented from returning by getting into the pockets and bulging them out so as to close the opening. These pockets are called the **sem-i-lu-nar** (half moon) **valves.**

7. The Left Auricle. — This cavity has four openings for as many pulmonary veins, which return the blood from the lungs, and one opening, through which the blood passes into the left ventricle.

8. The Left Ventricle. — This is similar to the right ventricle. The blood coming from the left auricle is prevented from returning by the **mi-tral valve** (so called from

62   PHYSIOLOGY FOR BEGINNERS.

its resemblance to a bishop's cap or " miter "). This valve consists of two flaps of membrane similar to those which compose the tricuspid valves. The contraction of the ventricle sends the blood into the **a-or-ta**, or great trunk of the arterial system, from which it is distributed throughout the body. The entrance to the aorta is guarded by a set of **semilunar valves**, like those on the right side of the heart.

9. **The Covering of the Heart.** — The heart is enclosed in a bag of fibrous membrane. This bag is lined with a serous membrane, which turns and covers the heart itself. The serous membrane secretes a fluid which keeps the surfaces moist and prevents friction. When this fluid is greatly increased in quantity, as is the case in some diseases, there is said to be "dropsy of the heart." The fibrous bag is called the **per-i-car-di-um** (around the heart).

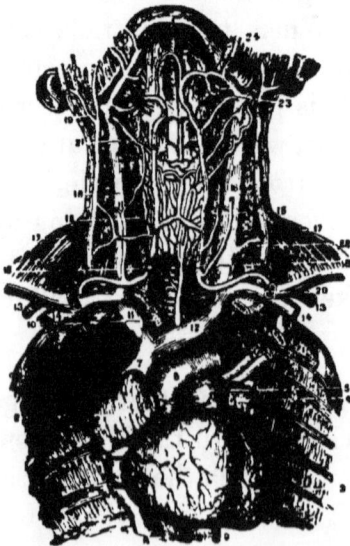

FIG. 9.

10. **The Structure of the Heart.** — The heart consists of muscular fibers interlaced and attached to fibrous rings, which surround the openings between the auricles and ventricles and the blood vessels. The cavities are lined with a serous membrane, which is a continuation of the inner coat of the blood vessels. This membrane is called the **en-do-car-di-um** (within the heart).

11. The Movements of the Heart. — We say the heart beats, or pulsates. This consists of a kind of wave motion, beginning with the auricles and ending with the ventricles. The muscular walls of the auricles first contract and force the blood into the ventricles, which are at that instant relaxed. Then the ventricles contract, and as the blood cannot go back into the auricles, being prevented by the valves, it is forced into the arteries. While the ventricles are contracting, the auricles are relaxed and filled with blood from the veins. The heart is suspended by the large blood vessels coming from its base, or upper end; but the lower end is free to move, and when the ventricles contract it is tilted so that it strikes the wall of the chest.

12. Rate of Pulsation. — The heart in a grown person beats, on an average, 70 times in a minute. In the newborn babe it beats from 130 to 140 times per minute, the rate gradually becoming less until old age. The heart beats a little faster in women than in men, faster during exercise and just after eating, and slower during sleep. Different conditions of disease cause variations. It has been known to beat but 20 times in a minute, and again as fast as 160 times per minute in the grown person.

13. Sounds of the Heart. — If the ear be placed over the chest, two distinct sounds may be heard, caused by the pulsation of the heart. One sound, which is called the *first sound*, is dull and caused by the muscular contraction of the ventricles. The other, called the *second sound*, is sharper and is caused by the shutting of the semilunar valves. Between the second and first sounds is an interval of silence. The physician uses an instrument called the *steth-o-scope*, which magnifies these sounds. He is thus enabled to discover diseases of the heart, for whenever there is any unnatural sound there is something wrong in the structure of the heart.

LESSON 22.

The Blood Vessels.

1. **Definition.** — The blood vessels are a set of elastic pipes, or tubes, which permit the blood to pass to every part of the body from the heart and back again to the heart. There are three kinds of blood vessels, **arteries**, **veins**, and **capillaries**. The *arteries* carry blood *away from* the heart. The *veins* carry blood *to the heart*. The capillaries are the fine tubes which connect the arteries to the veins throughout the tissues of the body.

2. **The A-or-ta.** — All of the arteries are branches of one great artery, which is called *the a-or-ta*. It is about one inch in diameter, and commences at the upper part of the left ventricle, curves over backward and toward the left, then descends along the left side of the spinal column as far as the fourth lumbar vertebra, where it divides to form the right and left *common iliac* arteries. A number of branches are given off along its course, these branches supplying the trunk of the body and the thoracic and abdominal organs with blood.

3. **Some of the Principal Arteries.** — It would be a great task to learn the names of all the arteries in the body, and unless you were a surgeon it would not be of importance to know them. But it will be interesting to

know the names of a few of the larger ones. First, the right and left coronary arteries supply the walls of the heart itself with blood. At the right of the curve of the aorta a short artery branches off, called the **in-nom-i-nate** artery. This divides into the **right ca-rot-id** and **right sub-cla-vi-an** arteries, the former supplying the right side of the head, and the latter the right shoulder and arm. The *left carotid* and *left subclavian* arteries branch off separately from the aorta.

The **gastric** artery supplies the stomach, the **hepatic** the liver, and the **splenic** the spleen. These three are branches of a short trunk which comes off from the aorta below the heart. The *superior* and *inferior* **mes-en-ter-ic** arteries supply the intestines. The aorta divides, as we have before stated, into the *right* and *left* **common iliac** arteries. These divide to form *internal* and *external iliac* arteries, the former supplying the parts about the pelvis, and the latter the lower limb. The external iliac takes the name of the **femoral** artery on the thigh.

4. Position of the Arteries. — The arteries are generally placed deep in the tissues of the body. Where they do come near the surface, it is always in a place that is naturally protected, as in the hollows formed by the angles of the limbs, the hollow of the neck, and similar places. Thus, you may feel the carotid artery pulsate in the side of the neck, the **temporal** in the hollow in front of the ear, the **pop-lit-e-al** behind the knee, and others in similar protected positions.

5. Structure of the Arteries. — The arteries are elastic tubes varying in size from nearly an inch in diameter down to a thickness but a little greater than a hair. The walls are composed of three layers, or coats. The outer and middle coats are composed of fibrous tissue, the latter containing muscular fibers, which are proportionally more abundant in the small arteries. The inner coat is a serous membrane, very smooth and thin. The outer coat is the strongest. If a string be tied very tightly around an artery, it will sever the middle and inner coat, leaving the outer coat uninjured. The outer coat is for strength, the middle for elasticity and contraction; and the inner makes a smooth surface for the flow of the blood.

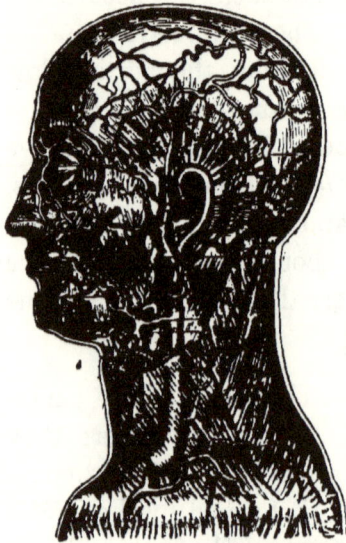

FIG. 10.

6. Branching of the Arteries. —When an artery divides to form t w o, each branch is smaller than the main one, but both taken together are larger than the main artery; so that the combined area of all the small arteries is much greater than the aorta, or main trunk. If this were not the case, the heart would have an immensely greater work to perform, for the friction would be greater. In many places the branches from a main artery join with other branches from the same artery. This is called **an-as-to-mos-ing**, a word which literally means " mouth to mouth." The surgeon is frequently required to tie a large artery, and in such cases these anastomosing branches carry the blood around and keep up the circulation.

7. The Veins.—These vessels carry back to the heart the blood that has been carried out through the system by the arteries. They are more numerous, but softer and weaker than the arteries. They are but slightly elastic, and when not filled with blood the walls collapse, or fall together. The deep veins accompany the arteries, there being gener-

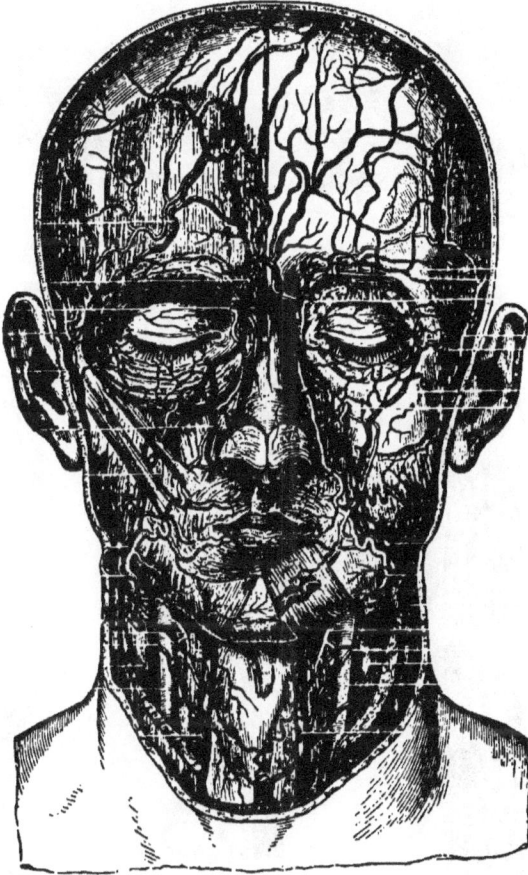

Fig. 11.

ally two to each artery, and take similar names. The superficial veins lie just beneath the skin, are smaller and very numerous. You may see on the back of your hand the ridges made by these superficial veins. You may by

pressure with your finger stop the flow of blood in one of
them.

8. **Structure of Veins.**—Like arteries, the walls are
composed of three coats. The middle coat is very weak

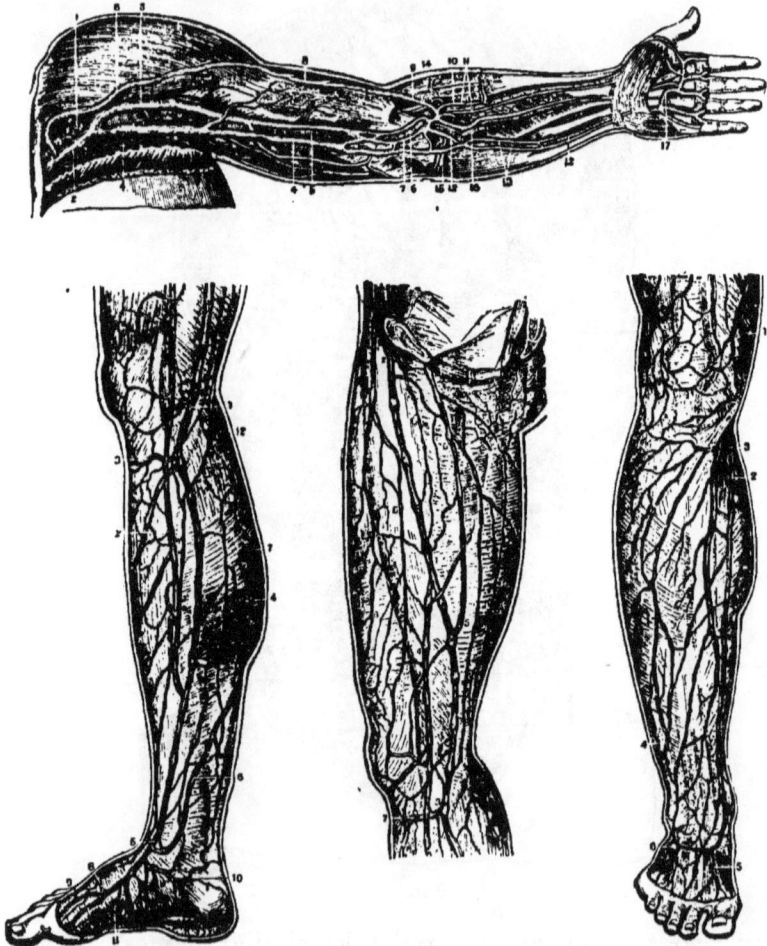

FIG. 12.

and has a very few muscular fibers. The inner layer contains folds in many places, called valves. These valves

permit the blood to pass in a direction *toward* the heart, but prevent its flow in the opposite direction.

9. **The Capillaries.** — The arteries get smaller and smaller and more numerous as they approach the tissues of the body which they supply with blood, and when not more than $\frac{1}{3000}$ of an inch in diameter they take the name of capillaries, from a Latin word meaning "hair." They are, indeed, smaller than hairs, but what they lack in size is made up in numbers. They are spread throughout the body so thickly that there are but few points on the body where a fine needle, if inserted, would not puncture one or more of them. There are none in the nails, hair, epidermis, and cornea of the eye. They consist of a single wall of transparent membrane, through which liquids and gases freely pass. You may then ask, Why does not the blood all leak out? There are two answers to this question. First, the blood is not a perfect liquid, being a liquid with myriads of solid little bodies floating in it. Second, the liquid part of the blood does leak through this membrane and thus furnishes material for building the tissues. The torn down tissues, also, in part pass back into the blood vessels through these capillary walls. The blood loses certain elements in passing from the arteries to the veins through the capillaries, and gains other elements. This change is shown by the difference of color. The blood in the arteries is a bright scarlet, and that in the veins is dark red. This is true of the vessels in general, but in the lungs it is reversed. The pulmonary artery carries dark blood, and after it has passed through the capillaries of the lungs, it appears in the pulmonary veins bright scarlet. We say the blood is purified by passing through the lungs and absorbing oxygen from the air.

LESSON 23.

The Blood and How it Circulates.

1. Quantity of Blood. — In a full-grown human body there are about two and a half gallons of blood, or, in other words, about one-eighth of the weight of the body.

2. Properties of Blood. — Blood is a little heavier than water, is salty to taste, and has an odor differing from that of any other substance. Its color, as we learned in the last lesson, is bright scarlet in the systemic arteries and darker in the systemic veins. In a few minutes after it leaves the body, it undergoes a peculiar change called **co-ag-u-la-tion**, or *clotting*. It separates into two portions, one thick, like jelly, and the other thin, like water. The jelly-like portion is much greater in quantity.

3. Composition of Fresh Blood. — To the unaided eye the blood appears as a simple red liquid, not unlike red ink. But if a little be spread thinly on a glass slide and examined with a good microscope, a number of little round bodies are seen floating in a clear liquid. These little bodies are called blood **cor-pus-cles** (little bodies), or blood cells. The majority of them appear faintly red or yellowish when seen singly, but when a number are heaped together, they have the deeper red color of the blood. Here and there among these red corpuscles may be seen some that are white or nearly colorless. The colorless liquid in which the corpuscles float is called **plasma**, or *liquor sanguinis*. It is composed of albuminous matter, mineral salts, and water. The red corpuscles contain a substance called **hem-o-glo-bin**. It contains iron and gives the blood its red color.

4. Composition of Coagulated Blood. — The watery part of clotted blood is called **se-rum**. The jelly-like part is called the **co-ag-u-lum**, or *clot*. It consists of a stringy substance called fibrin and corpuscles, which seem to be simply entangled in it. By taking a portion of clot and shaking in a bottle of clean water, then pouring off the red liquid and repeating this many times, a white stringy substance is left. This is the fibrin. The water is reddened by the corpuscles, which are dissolved in it.

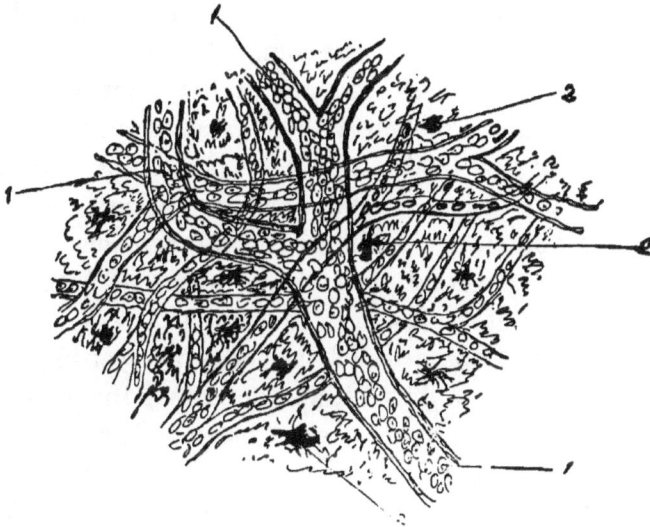

FIG. 13.

5. Importance of Coagulation. — The cause of coagulation is not certainly known, but its importance to the animal is undoubted. It is nature's method of stopping bleeding. The blood by coagulating closes the severed vessels, and thus stops the flow from the wound. Unless a very large blood vessel be severed, there is seldom a case of bleeding to death either in man or animals. In birds coagulation takes place almost instantly after leaving the blood vessels.

6. The Use of the Corpuscles. — The red corpuscles carry oxygen from the lungs to the tissues of the body. The oxygen is a part of the air we breathe, and is essential to all living things. The hemoglobin of the red corpuscles unites with the oxygen, and in this manner the latter is carried to the tissues of the body. The white corpuscles are probably concerned in the growth and repair of the tissues.

7. The Course of the Blood in the Body. — Starting with the capillaries throughout the tissues of the body, let us trace the blood in its ceaseless round. From the capillaries it flows into the small branches of the veins, from these into larger, and again into larger branches, until the heart is reached by two main trunks. These empty the blood into the main auricle. From the right auricle it flows into the right ventricle. From the right ventricle into the pulmonary artery, and through its numerous branches to the capillaries of the lungs. Thus far it is dark, or venous blood. In the capillaries of the lungs it receives oxygen and gives up carbon dioxide, and appears in the pulmonary veins as bright red, or arterial blood. The pulmonary veins empty it into the left auricle. From here it passes to the left ventricle. From the left ventricle it is forced into the aorta, and from thence into all its branches and branches of branches, until the capillaries of the body are again reached.

A kind of special circulation exists in the liver. All the blood which has been distributed to the stomach, spleen, and intestines is gathered up by veins which unite to form the **por-tal vein**, which enters the liver, and there divides again into many branches. This blood is then gathered up by the hepatic veins in the liver, and emptied into the *inferior vena cava,* or lower great trunk of the venous system. This course of the blood is called the **portal circulation.**

8. Cause of Circulation. — The main cause of circulation is the pumping force of the heart. This force is felt in the smallest arteries as a pulsation, or beat. Every time the heart beats there is a pulsation in all the arteries. Although the pulsation is not usually to be perceived in the capillaries and veins, yet the pressure produced by the pumping of the heart is sufficient to send the blood through the capillaries into the veins. Muscular contraction in the walls of the arteries, the elasticity of the

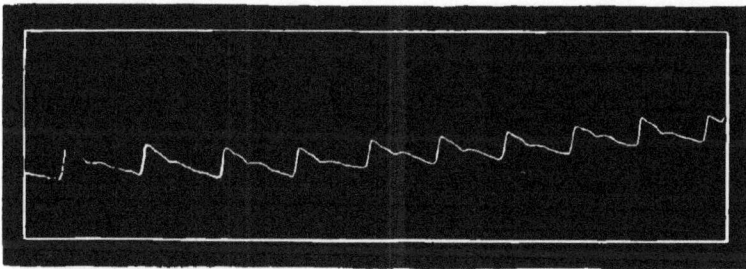

FIG. 14.

arteries, the pressure of the moving muscles of the body upon the veins, aided by their valves, all have their effect in aiding the action of the heart.

9. The "Pulse-writer." — The physician feels the pulse of the patient to ascertain how the heart is beating, and to know the force of the circulating blood current, for these are important facts in studying the nature of the disease. An instrument has been invented which writes down the condition of the circulatory system. It consists of a lever so arranged that the pulse in the wrist may move it up and down freely. At the same time the point of the lever is made to press upon a piece of smoked paper, which is made to move along at a regular rate by clockwork. In this way the lever is made to write a wavy line as shown in the picture, which is an exact copy of the writing made by the pulse of the author of this book. Variations in these curves show variations in force, frequency, and regularity of the heart-beats, and the degree of resistance in the arteries, points of great value to the physician.

10. **Rate of Circulation.** — A given portion of blood may make the complete circuit of the body; that is, from veins to right side of heart, to lungs, back to left side of heart, to the arteries, and thence through the capillaries to the veins again from whence it started, in the short space of twenty-four seconds. It is estimated that the entire amount of blood in a man's body makes a complete circuit every two minutes.

LESSON 24.

The Lymphatics.

1. **What are Lymphatics?** — They are a system of vessels and glands which aid the circulatory system. The vessels carry a fluid called **lymph.**

2. **Lymphatic Vessels.** — These are minute, delicate, transparent tubes, with valves in their interior, giving them a beaded or knotted appearance. They are found in nearly every part of the body, being more numerous than the veins.

3. **Thoracic Duct and Right Lymphatic Duct.** — All the lymphatic vessels of the body, except those of the right

side of the head, neck and chest, right arm, lung and upper surface of the liver, unite and empty their contents into one common trunk — *the thoracic duct.* It lies along the front of the spinal column, extending from the second lumbar vertebra to the seventh cervicle. It is about 18 inches long, and one-quarter of an inch thick. The lower end is a kind of bag called the *receptacle of the chyle,* and the upper end empties into the left subclavian vein. All those lymphatic vessels which do not empty into the thoracic duct form a common duct about one inch in length, called the *right lymphatic duct.* It empties into the right subclavian vein.

4. **The Lacteals.** — Those lymphatics which terminate in the villi of the intestines (see Lesson 14) are called **lacteals,** from a Latin word meaning *milk,* because during digestion they are filled with a milk-white fluid, the **chyle.** They empty the chyle into the thoracic duct, where it mingles with the lymph, and finally enters the general blood current.

5. **The Lymphatic Glands.** — These are small bodies, varying in size from that of a grain of wheat to the size of an almond. They are found in various parts of the body in the course of the lymphatic vessels. They are especially numerous just beneath the skin under the arms, in the side of the neck, and in the groin. They sometimes become swollen when there is a wound near them, and often are enlarged in scrofulous persons. A lymphatic vessel passes into each one, divides into branches, which unite again as they pass out. Their use is not certainly known.

6. **Uses of the Lymphatics.** — As we have learned, the tissues are constantly being torn down and built up anew

by the blood. The plasma of the blood passes through the
walls of the capillaries, and is used in forming new cells.
The material of the old cells is removed in part by flowing
back again into the capillaries. There is thus a current set-
ting both ways, one out of the blood vessels into the tissues,
the other into the blood vessels. But wherever there are
capillaries there are lymphatics, and it is supposed that
when there is more plasma passed through the capillaries
than is necessary for building and rebuilding the tissues, it
is taken in by the lymphatics and thus returned to the
blood. Probably a part of the waste material is also
carried away by the lymphatics. The lymphatic vessels
then seem to be an aid to the circulatory system.

LESSON 25.

How to Care for the Circulatory System.

1. **Effects of Cold and Heat.** — Cold temporarily increases the circulation, but, if continued, checks it unless
counterbalanced by exercise and stimulants, which for a
short time may keep it up. Heat increases the circulation.
but when too great lessens it. *All extremes of cold and
heat are injurious, and one should avoid exposure to extreme
conditions as much as possible.* Comfortable clothing and
shelter tend to prolong life. Coldness of feet and hands
is generally due to imperfect circulation of the blood to the
extremities, and this deficiency of circulation is frequently
brought on by exposure of these parts to the cold in the
first place. *The feet especially should be kept warm and
dry.*

2. **Exercise and Circulation.** — Place your finger on your wrist and count the pulsations of the radial artery for a minute or two. Then exercise vigorously for several minutes, and count again. You will observe an increase in the number of pulsations per minute. The heart beats more rapidly during exercise, and the blood is sent more freely to all parts of the body. The movements of the muscles also help the blood to move in the veins, and the waste and repair of the tissues goes on more rapidly, thus creating a demand for more blood in the capillaries. When the feet begin to feel cold a vigorous and constant working of the toes will soon make them warm, because of the increased amount of blood sent to them. Severe and long-continued exercise may cause sudden failure of the heart or rupture of a blood vessel.

3. **Effects of Nervous Shocks on the Circulation.** — The circulation of the blood is controlled by the nervous system, and any cause which over-excites or disturbs the nerves has an injurious effect on the heart and blood vessels. Strong emotions, as fear, anger, and grief, cause irregular action of the heart, and consequently of the blood vessels. Every one knows how fear causes paleness, and embarrassment and anger cause blushing or redness of the face. This is due to the nerves causing contractions and relaxations of the muscular fibers of the smaller arteries. *The cause of nervous shocks and excitements can many times be avoided. It is physiologically wrong to frighten people, and giving way to fits of anger is at the expense of injury to the circulatory system. The lives of politicians and men in public life are often shortened by the excitement under which they live.*

4. Bleeding from Veins and Arteries. — When a vein is severed the, blood flows in a steady stream and is a little darker in appearance; when an artery is severed the blood flows in spurts or jets and is brighter in color. As the bloods flows *towards* the heart in the veins, if the bleeding be considerable it should be stopped by a bandage placed on the side of the wound farthest from the heart. As the blood in the arteries is flowing *from* the heart, the bandage should be placed on the side nearest the heart. No time should be lost in case the blood flows in jets, as a great and perhaps serious loss of blood will soon take place from an ar-

FIG. 15.

tery. A handkerchief, or towel tied loosely around the limb and twisted with a stick, as shown in the picture, will quickly arrest the bleeding until a surgeon can be called. In case of a large artery the surgeon will be obliged to find the severed ends of the artery and tie them.

5. Alcohol and the Circulatory Organs. — Alcohol at first causes the heart to beat more rapidly and with greater force, sending more blood to the surface of the body. This causes a sensation of warmth and in cold weather seems agreeable, and it is thought by many to be very beneficial. But a great mistake is made. The blood being sent to the surface soon loses its heat by radiation and evaporation from the skin, and the person thus rapidly losing the animal heat of the body is less able to resist external cold. *The experience of travelers in cold regions of the earth proves that alcohol renders men* *less able to withstand the cold.* Again, some think that alcoholic drinks are excellent in hot weather. Here, again, they are mistaken. Alcohol does cool the body, but it does it by sending blood to the surface and increasing the flow of perspiration which by its rapid evaporation causes a sensation of coolness. But this unnatural stimulus to the glands of the skin tends to exhaust and weaken them.

Frequent stimulations by alcoholic drinks cause permanent enlargement of the capillaries. The red face of the drunkard is caused in this way. The heart also becomes weakened by frequent excitements and is liable to rapid failure at about the middle age of life. It is a well-known fact that habitual drinkers nearly always die when attacked by such epidemics as cholera, smallpox, etc. It is because the circulatory system is not equal to the task of throwing the poison of these diseases out of the system.

6. Tobacco and the Circulatory Organs. — Doctors frequently speak of a " tobacco heart," or a " smoker's heart." What do they mean by these expressions? *Tobacco in some persons especially is apt to cause irregular action of the heart, sometimes called palpitation of the heart. Such fits of palpitation are not only very disagreeable, but there is actual danger of complete failure of the heart, and repeated attacks are followed by derangements of other organs from want of proper nourishment by the great renewer of life — the blood.*

LESSON 26.

Review of the Circulatory System.

1. Where is the heart? Describe it as to size and shape. Where can you feel it beating?

2. How many cavities in the heart? Name them. What kind of blood in the cavities of the right side? In those of the left side? Which cavities have the thickest walls?

3. Where are the semilunar valves? What do they resemble? Where is the tricuspid valve? The mitral valve? What kind of blood flows through the tricuspid valve?

4. What is the pericardium? What lines the cavities of the heart?

5. How many times does the heart beat in a minute? What causes the sounds of the heart?

6. Tell all you can about the aorta. What is the main trunk of the arterial system? How do arteries differ from veins?

7. What large artery may be felt pulsating in the neck? What parts does it supply with blood? What main artery supplies the arm?

8. How many coats have the arteries? Which is the strongest? Which one contains muscular fibers?

9. What are the capillaries? How large are they?

10. How much blood in a man of ordinary size? What is the color, taste, and odor of blood?

11. What change takes place in blood after it leaves the body? What is fresh blood composed of?

12. What is plasma? What substance in red corpuscles contains iron?

13. State the differences in the composition of fresh and coagulated blood. What advantage in coagulation?

14. Of what use are the red corpuscles? Trace a particle of blood from the right to the left side of the heart, naming the vessels and organs it must pass through. In the same manner trace a particle from the left to the right side.

15. Does the pulmonary artery contain arterial blood? What is the portal circulation?

16. What makes the blood circulate? Explain how the physician can tell about the beating of the heart by feeling the patient's pulse at the wrist.

17. How long does it take for any particular portion of blood to complete the round of the circulation?

18. What are lymphatics? Describe the thoracic duct. What are the lacteals? Where are the lymphatic glands? Uses of the lymphatics?

19. How does extreme cold and heat affect the circulatory organs? What is the effect of exercise on circulation? Why is it important to keep the feet warm? Why is undue excitement injurious?

20. Where would you tie the bandage in case of a wounded artery? How would you know it was an artery and not a vein?

21. How does alcohol affect the circulation? Does alcohol make one really warmer? How does tobacco affect the heart?

22. The pupil must bear in mind that the heart, arteries, capillaries, and veins form a completely closed chamber, or rather a cave, or house with many chambers and passages all connected together, but completely closed against the outside world. To make this clearer, let us suppose ourselves as small as a blood corpuscle and placed in one

of the cavities of the heart; we could travel through all the veins, arteries, and capillaries and back again to the heart, without finding an opening large enough through which to escape. Yet, strange to say, the white corpuscles have been known to escape through the capillaries and get out among the tissues. They do this, not by finding or making an opening, but by being drawn out to an exceedingly small thread and recovering their shape again on the opposite side. This is truly a wonderful phenomenon.

LESSON 27.

The Machinery of Breathing.

1. Importance of Breathing. — We all know that when an animal stops breathing it dies ; that is, that air is necessary to life. We can live without food for several days, but the stoppage of respiration, or breathing, for a few minutes is death. All animals breathe, that is, take in the oxygen of the air in some way. In the lowest forms the little oxygen which is mixed with the water is sufficient to support life, and in some it simply circulates through the animal with the water in which they live. In others it passes through them in a set of tubes which open at various places on the surface of their bodies. All higher animals, however, have a *larynx*, a *trachea*, *bronchial tubes*, and *lungs*. These are the organs of respiration.

2. The Larynx. — The pharynx, which has already been described, receives air from either the passages of the nose or from the mouth. From the pharynx the air

passes into the larynx, which is a short tube, or box, composed of nine pieces of cartilage held together by fibrous
membrane. You can feel the **thy-roid** (shield-like) cartilage of the larynx in your neck. It is the prominent,
hard lump, sometimes called " Adam's Apple." The thy-
roid cartilage forms the greater part of the larynx. The
lower and narrowest part is formed by the **cri-coid** (ring-
like) cartilage. This cartilaginous box has a peculiar lid
at the top called the **ep-i-glot-tis.** The other six cartilages
are small and help form the back part of the larynx.

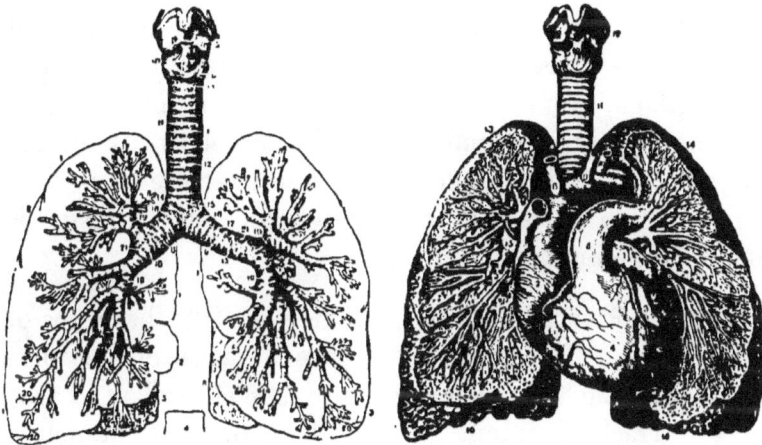

FIG. 17.

The epiglottis is somewhat like a trap-door ; it stands open
to admit air, except when food or drink is being swallowed. Then it is closed to prevent the food from entering the larynx. Sometimes when we attempt to talk or
breathe while swallowing, a little food or drink gets into
the larynx (" goes the wrong way," we say), and violent
coughing is caused.

3. **The Organ of Voice.** — The larynx is the organ of
voice as well as a part of the breathing machinery. There

are two ligaments covered with mucous membrane stretched across the sides of the interior of the larynx; these are called **vocal cords.** Various degrees of tightening of these cords cause variations in the sound made by the air being forced through the larynx from the lungs. The sound is modified also by the variations in the size of the opening between the cords, which is made to change by muscles in the walls of the larynx.

4. **The Trachea.** — The trachea, commonly called the *wind-pipe,* extends from the larynx downward about four inches, and then divides, or forks, to form the bronchial tubes. It is a peculiar tube made up of incomplete rings of cartilage, from sixteen to twenty in number, joined together by fibrous membrane. This arrangement secures the proper amount of flexibility, and is at the same time rigid enough to remain an open tube. Its diameter is about three-fourths of an inch.

5. **The Bronchial Tubes.** — These are the branches of the trachea. The picture will give an idea of the form of these branches. The structure is very similar to that of the trachea, except in the very smallest branches, where the cartilage rings are wanting.

6. **Mucous Membrane.** — A continuous layer of mucous membrane lines the larynx, trachea, and bronchial tubes. That in the trachea and bronchial tubes is thickly set with cells containing fine, hair-like projections, called **cil-i-a.** They have the peculiar power of moving or waving together, like a field of grain when swayed by the wind. This motion is most forcible in the direction of the mouth, so that small particles placed on them are carried upward. In this way dust taken in with the air

is in part expelled. The mucus, secreted by the mucous membrane, serves as a protection from the irritating influence of the air.

7. The Lungs. — The entire cavity of the chest, except the small space occupied by the heart and its blood vessels and the esophagus, is filled by the *two lungs*. The picture gives a very good idea of their shape — larger at the lower part and tapering upward to the neck. They are a light pink or rose color, getting darker with age. They are very light in weight, by reason of the air they contain. A piece of lung tissue of an animal that has once breathed will always float in water.

8. Structure of the Lungs. — Try to form an idea of their structure by imagining a hollow tree with a great number of branches, each branch hollow and terminating in a little bag of membrane. The trunk of the tree represents the trachea, the branches the bronchial tubes, and the little bags of membrane at the tips of the smallest branches are the **air cells.** Now imagine twined with this tree, another somewhat similar in shape, but containing a red fluid. This would represent the **pulmonary artery** and its branches. Suppose the ends of the branches of this last tree were continuous with the branches of several similar trees. These would represent the **pulmonary veins.** The smallest branches of the veins and arteries are the capillaries of the lungs. They form a dense network around the air cells. All these tubes and branches are connected by a fine, fibrous tissue, and lymphatic vessels also penetrate every part. The amount of surface of the interior of the air cells, if spread out, would be very great. It is estimated to be as much as fifteen hundred square feet.

9. **The Pleura.** — The cavity of the chest is lined with a delicate, serous membrane, which turns and covers the lungs, and thus forms a complete bag. The inner surfaces secrete a fluid which keeps them moist and prevents friction when the lungs move in the chest. This membrane is called the *pleura.* When it is inflamed, the disease is known as *pleurisy.*

LESSON 28.

How and Why we Breathe.

1. **Respiration.** — This is only another name for the process of breathing. It consists of two acts, taking in of air, which is called **inspiration,** and expelling the air, which is called **expiration.** Respiration is an involuntary process. We can hold our breath for a time, but in a few seconds an exceedingly uncomfortable feeling compels us to take in air. When an animal has ceased to breathe it is dead, or will be in a very short time. It is true that there are some cases where respiration has apparently stopped and the person appears to be dead, and yet after the lapse of sometimes many hours he comes to life again. In these cases of "suspended animation;" as they are called, breathing goes on to a very slight extent, although unperceived.

2. **How the Air enters the Lungs.** — The air, like all other matter, has weight. The entire amount of atmosphere presses upon every square inch of surface, by reason of its weight, with a force of about fifteen pounds. If you immerse an empty bottle in water the water will

rush in until it is filled. All objects on the earth are immersed in the atmosphere. The moment you create a cavity, air rushes in just as water into the bottle. You are all familiar with a pair of bellows. It consists of two boards lying close together, with their edges joined by some flexible material, as leather. When you pull the boards apart you create a cavity between them, and the air rushes in at the hole in one of the boards. The air enters the lungs in a similar manner. The cavity of the chest is enlarged in the act of inspiration in two ways: *First, by the descent of the diaphragm.* This is a muscular partition across the body, dividing the cavity of the chest from the cavity of the abdomen. When at rest the diaphragm is convex on the upper side. The central portion is a flat tendon, and when the fibers of the muscular part contract they pull the center down. This increases the size of the chest cavity. *Second, by the elevation of the ribs.* You will notice in the picture of the skeleton that the ribs all incline downward from the spinal column. When the front ends of the ribs are raised they stand out farther from the spinal column, and thus enlarge the cavity of the chest. The muscles between the ribs and certain others of the back, neck, and shoulders all aid in raising the ribs.

As the air enters the lungs all the little air cells fill out, and the lungs are increased in bulk corresponding to the increased size of the chest cavity.

3. **How the Air leaves the Lungs.** — The air is forced out of the lungs by the elastic reaction of the various tissues. When you bend a stick and let go, it springs back with great force of elasticity. Now, when the diaphragm is drawn down by its muscular fibers, it presses

the organs in the abdomen against the elastic walls of the latter, which spring back again when the muscular force is relaxed. The ribs are returned to their position by the elasticity of their cartilages. The tissues of the lungs which have been stretched by the inrushing air resume their original conditions and aid in drawing out the air.

4. **Rate of Breathing.** — A grown person breathes, on an average, eighteen times per minute. Exercise and other circumstances increase this rate. Children breathe more rapidly than adults. A man will breathe about nine million times in a year.

5. **Effect of Breathing on the Air.** — The air consists of about four parts **nitrogen** gas, one part **oxygen** gas, and about four one-hundredths part of **carbon dioxide,** or carbonic acid gas, with a small amount of vapor of water. When it comes out of the lungs a chemical analysis shows that it has lost something and gained something. It has four or five parts less of oxygen, and about four parts more carbon dioxide. It has also an increased amount of moisture and is considerably warmer than before. The red corpuscles have absorbed some of the oxygen of the air and carried it to the tissues, there to be given up for use in the growth and repair of the body. The carbon dioxide is a result of the destruction of the tissues which is constantly going on and is thrown out of the body as waste matter.

6. **Voice.** — The sound made by air from the lungs driven forcibly through the larynx is called *voice*. These sounds are variously modified, separated, and joined together in the mouth, by the tongue, teeth, and lips. This joining and separating of sounds is called *articula-*

tion. Many animals have voice, but cannot articulate sounds. A few, as the parrot and raven, have been taught to articulate quite distinctly. About forty distinct sounds are used in speaking the English language. Some animals, as insects, make their characteristic sounds by the rubbing together of their wings, or by the leg against the wing. Such sounds are difficult to distinguish from vocal sounds, that is, sounds made through the larynx.

LESSON 29.

How to Care for the Breathing Organs.

1. **The Need of Pure Air.** — By *pure air*, we mean air that has the proper proportion of oxygen, nitrogen, and watery vapor, and contains no injurious gases or other substances that would injure the system. The blood needs a certain amount of oxygen at all times to maintain its proper condition and make it fit to nourish the body. If the air be mixed with other gases the amount of oxygen will be to that extent lessened. The carbon dioxide given off in respiration is not injurious in itself, but if it exists in an unusual amount it displaces too much of the oxygen. But the amount seldom reaches an injurious degree. The greater danger lies in substances in the air which are injurious in themselves. The lungs throw off a certain amount of dead matter (organic matter), which, if inhaled again, is injurious. A poisonous gas is often given off from cast-iron stoves when not properly constructed. Factories sometimes produce injurious gases, which escape into the atmosphere. Decaying animal bodies and vegetable mat-

ter produce gases which are injurious when inhaled. *It is very important then that we inhale pure air.*

2. The Need of Moisture in the Air. — All air contains some water in the form of an invisible vapor. This can be shown by a simple experiment which you should try when you have an opportunity. Fill a dry glass tumbler with ice cold water and place it in a warm room. In a few minutes the outside of the glass will be quite moist, the water even collecting in drops and running down the sides of the glass. In this case the cold glass condenses the moisture of the air. Too much moisture in the air makes breathing difficult, as the oxygen is diluted and greater effort is required to get the proper amount. The air then seems heavy, although it is really lighter, as the watery vapor is lighter than the air. On the other hand, very dry air irritates the mucous membrane of the air passages. A vessel of water placed on the stove, will, by its evaporation, increase the moisture of the air in a room where it has become too dry.

3. Dust in the Air. — The air always contains more or less solid matter in the form of dust. We cannot see this dust unless it is illuminated by a strong light. Sometimes when the sun shines through a small opening in the room, we see bright bands of dust particles. When the dust is considerable in quantity, it irritates the lungs and tends to produce disease. *Floors and furniture should be kept perfectly clean, and rooms should be frequently opened to keep them from accumulating dust.*

4. Germs of Disease in the Air. — The microscope has revealed the fact that the air may contain various kinds of germs (seeds) of very minute plants, and it is believed that nearly all diseases are caused by these germs getting into the blood and there growing and multiplying. This is believed to be true, at least, of the contagious diseases, as smallpox, diphtheria, cholera, etc. Physicians and surgeons now take great pains to prevent these germs from getting into the blood through wounds, and to rid the air of them. The treatment of such diseases is therefore more successful now than formerly. The air in the immediate neighborhood of sick persons is apt to contain germs of disease which will affect others. Many of these germs enter the blood through the lungs. *Filth and dirt of all kinds favor the growth of injurious germs, hence cleanliness is important.* Disinfectants are substances which destroy these germs.

5. **Ventilation.** — That we may not breathe the same air over and over, there should be a constant circulation of air. The air that leaves the lungs, as we have learned, is warmer, and rises out of the way while we inhale a fresh amount; but if we are in a tight room, where this once-breathed air cannot escape and a proper supply of fresh air cannot enter, this bad air mingles with the pure air, and we are compelled to breathe it over again. A room that permits the ready escape of foul air and the entrance of fresh air is said to be *ventilated.*

6. **"Catching Cold."** — A cold is a peculiar condition of the mucous membrane, usually of the air passages, caused by sudden or great cooling of the body. This cooling or lowering of the temperature of the body is usually caused by draughts of cool air. Rooms that are improperly ventilated expose persons to draughts of air which may cause a severe cold that may result in some serious disease of the respiratory organs, as pneumonia,

bronchitis, and even consumption. There is very little danger of taking cold in a draught if one is exercising, because the exercise keeps up the body temperature; but when sitting still in a strong draught the danger is great. *When tired and heated from exercise one should be very careful not to sit still where there is a strong current of air.*

7. **Proper Ventilation.** — A room is properly ventilated when the fresh air has free access and the foul air is permitted to pass out, in such a way that no one is exposed to a draught of cool air. In a room with a fire the cold air should come in near the source of the heat and become warmed before it strikes the persons in the room, and the warmed air should be permitted to escape at a point farthest from the source of the heat.

8. **Exercise and Respiration.** — That kind of exercise which brings into use the muscles of the arms and chest is especially beneficial to the breathing organs.

Breathing exercises like the following should be taken every day: Stand erect, throw the shoulders back, and slowly inhale; then slowly exhale. Repeat several times in succession. *Inhale through the nose, never through the mouth. The mouth should always be kept closed when we are not eating, talking, or singing.* The nasal passages warm the air, and catch much of the dust that would otherwise enter the lungs.

9. **Alcohol and the Breathing Organs.** — Alcohol causes an increased flow of blood to the capillaries. The lungs are thus overfilled and the exchange of gases rendered imperfect. Excessive use of alcoholic drinks tends to thicken the mucous membrane and render it less sensitive. The drunkard always has a wheezy, or thick and unnatural voice.

10. Tobacco *frequently irritates the mucous membranes of the air passages, and by its bad effect on the nervous system injuriously affects all the organs of the body, and among them those of the respiratory system.*

LESSON 30.

Review of the Respiratory System.

1. What gas is necessary for all animal life? What are the organs of respiration?

2. Describe the larynx in your own language. What happens when we say the food or water goes the wrong way? What is Adam's Apple?

3. Where are the vocal cords? What is the use of the epiglottis? What is the organ of voice?

4. What is the use of the trachea? What are the uses of the cartilage rings in the trachea? What are the bronchial tubes?

5. What lines the larynx, trachea, and bronchial tubes? What are cilia? What is the use of them?

6. What is the use of the mucous membrane? Why are the lungs so light in weight?

7. What and where are the air cells? What are they the terminations of? What surrounds the air cells? The capillaries of the lungs, which are the terminations of the pulmonary artery and the beginnings of the pulmonary veins. Here the exchange of gases is made. The oxygen passes through the walls of the air cells, and through the capillary walls, and into the red corpuscles of the blood, and the carbon dioxide passes in a similar manner from the blood to the interior of the air cells.

8. What is the pleura? What other membrane that you have learned about is it similar to in structure and use?

9. What is the difference between inspiration and expiration? What is the difference between inspired air and expired air?

10. What makes the air enter the lungs? What drives it out? How fast do you breathe?

11. What is the difference between voice and articulation? Has a dog voice? Has a katy-did voice? No, its music is instrumental, not vocal. The music of the canary bird is vocal music.

12. Do we need pure air for breathing? Why? Is very dry air injurious? Why? What is the effect of dust in the air? What are disinfectants?

13. What is ventilation? What is the objection to sitting by an open window when the air outside is cooler than that inside of the room? How do we " catch cold"?

14. What can you say of breathing exercises? Of alcohol and tobacco in connection with the respiratory system?

LESSON 31.

The Skin.

1. **Definition.** — The skin is the layer of tissue which, like a tight-fitting but elastic garment, covers all parts of the body exposed to the air, except those parts which are covered with mucous membrane. It is a garment easily cleaned, and renews itself as fast as it wears out.

It consists of two principal layers, the *epidermis, cuticle* or *scarf skin,* and the *derma* or *true skin.*

2. **The Epidermis.** — This is the outer layer of the skin. It is composed of what is called horny tissue and has no blood vessels nor nerves. It again is composed of two layers, the outer one of hard, flattened cells like scales. These are continually coming off, and their places

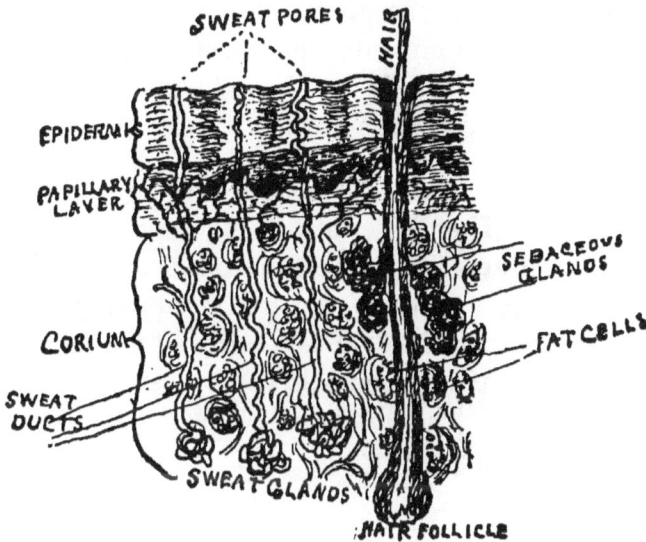

FIG. 18.

are taken by new ones from the layer beneath. In the scalp these scales sometimes accumulate in considerable quantity and are known as " *dandruff.*" The deep layer consists of rounded cells which contain a coloring matter called the *pigment* of the skin. In those people called *albinos* this pigment is entirely absent. In persons of fair complexion there is very little pigment. In the negro and other dark races it is very abundant. When it is found thicker in spots it produces "*freckles.*"

3. The Derma, or True Skin. — This again is composed
of two layers; the outer one is called the *papillary layer.*
It consists of little elevations very close together. In the
palm of the hand they are in rows, making the peculiar
lines we see. These little projections contain the extremities of the nerves and capillaries of the skin. The next
layer is called the *corium*. It is tough and elastic, and
consists of bundles of fibers, some of which are muscular
fibers, mingled with the glands of the skin, fat, and the
hair follicles. The muscular fibers contract when exposed
to cold, and draw the skin into little lumps. This appearance is often called "*goose flesh.*"

4. Uses of the Skin. — The skin is the great *protector*
of the body. The epidermis, being without nerves, is
insensible, and acts as a protector from the air and other
objects. It also prevents the too rapid escape of heat
and lessens evaporation. The entire skin also protects
the muscles and nerves beneath, and prevents evaporation
and loss of heat. The numerous glands in the skin serve
an important purpose which will be discussed in the
following lesson.

LESSON 32.

Hair, Nails, and Glands of the Skin.

1. The Hair. — The hair is really composed of the
same kind of material as the epidermis of the skin. The
outer portion consists of scales overlapping like shingles
on a roof, but very small and close together, so that it
requires a high power of the microscope to show it so.
Beneath this is a layer of long cells which contain a *pig-*

ment, or coloring matter, and in the center is the *pith,* consisting of cells and air spaces.

2. How Hair grows. — A hair grows from the root end. When you pull one out there is still left, in a little bag called the *hair follicle,* a little germ which grows to produce a new hair. This hair follicle is sometimes in the skin and sometimes beneath it. When hair becomes gray the pigment matter disappears, and air takes the place of it in the cells, giving the white appearance.

3. Uses of the Hair. — The hair protects the parts which it covers from extremes of heat and cold. It also helps to lessen the force of blows or contact with objects, and carries off the sweat.

4. The Nails. — The nails, like the hair, are composed of the same material as the epidermis of the skin. A nail grows from the root and under surface, the body of the nail being pushed out as the new growth advances. The free end and upper surface of the nail is insensible, as it contains no nerves; but the tissue at the root and just beneath is very sensitive, so that intense pain is produced when a nail is crushed or pulled out. You can readily name the uses of the nails. Were they absent we could not pick up small objects, and the ends of the fingers and toes would be in continual danger of injury.

5. The Sweat Glands. — These are very numerous in all parts of the skin. They consist of very fine tubes, extending from the surface to the deepest part of the skin and sometimes beneath it. The lower end is coiled up in a bunch, and the opening at the upper end is called a *pore.* These glands secrete the *perspiration,* or sweat.

When the body becomes warm in a heated atmosphere, or by physical exercise, these glands pour out an abundant supply of perspiration, which evaporates, and this evaporation cools the body. A large amount of waste material is also thrown off in this way.

6. The Oil Glands. — These are found to some extent in the skin of the entire body, but are much more numerous on the scalp and face. They consist of clusters of little bags in the deep layer of the skin or just beneath it. Each gland has a duct, which opens either on the surface or by the side of the root of a hair. They secrete an oil which serves to keep the skin and hair soft and protects them from the perspiration. The oil is carried by capillary attraction along the entire length of the longest hair.

LESSON 33.

Mucous and Serous Membrane.

1. Where is Mucous Membrane? — In this book we have already, in several places, talked about mucous and serous membranes, so that this lesson will be a kind of review. The mucous membrane is really one continuous covering or lining, although it has very many parts. *It lines or covers all surfaces that are exposed to the air and that are not covered with skin.* It lines all the *respiratory organs*, which means that beginning with the cavity of the nose, it extends into the pharynx, larynx, trachea, bronchial tubes large and small, and finally into the air cells of the lungs. It lines the *alimentary canal*, which means, that beginning with the mouth, it lines the pharynx, esophagus, stomach, small and large intestines, and all the ducts of glands which pour their secretion into this alimentary canal, as the ducts of the salivary glands, the pancreas, and the liver. There are also many cavities in the bones of the head which connect with the cavities of the nose and pharynx, and they are also lined with mucous membrane.

2. **What is Mucous Membrane?** — It consists of one or more layers of cells of different shapes and sizes. The cells of the outer layer are continually coming off just like those of the epidermis. The shapes of the cells differ in different parts of the body. Figure 19 shows the form of the cells of the mucous membrane of the trachea. It contains **cilia,** which were described in a former lesson. The outer layer has no blood vessels, and with some exceptions no nerves, but the deeper layer is abundantly supplied with both.

3. **Uses of Mucous Membrane.** — It serves to protect the delicate parts which it covers. It secretes a fluid called **mucus.** This keeps its surface always moist, and protects the parts from the air and from dust and gases in the atmosphere. In the alimentary canal it prevents its walls from adhering together and aids in the passage of food through it.

4. **Where is Serous Membrane?** — There are many surfaces in the body which are not exposed to air, as the surface of the brain, the outside of the stomach, liver, and other organs of the abdomen, the heart and lungs. All such surfaces are covered, and the cavities which contain these organs are lined with serous membrane. In the chest that part which covers the lungs and lines the

walls is called the pleura, and that which covers the heart, the *pericardium*. In the abdominal cavity it is all in one continuous piece, and is called the **per-i-to-ne-um.** A continuous serous membrane lines the heart and blood vessels. That covering the brain and spinal cord will be mentioned when we come to describe those parts.

5. What is Serous Membrane? — It resembles mucous membrane in structure. The cells are usually flattened, and the surface is always smooth and shining and kept constantly moist with *serous fluid* secreted by the membrane.

6. Uses of Serous Membrane. — They are for the prevention of friction when one part moves on another. With every movement of the body the organs are shaken and slide about in their cavities, and if it were not for this smooth, moist membrane, they would be injured.

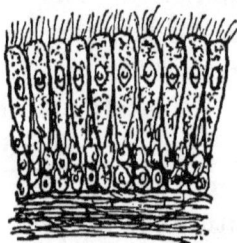

FIG. 19.

LESSON 34.

Secretion, Excretion, and Absorption.

1. Definitions. — Here are three words which we must know the meaning of, as used in Physiology. The living body is a great machine, or rather a great laboratory or workshop, where many processes of manufacture are going on. For example, the food is digested, and for this purpose certain fluids are necessary. The body makes these fluids out of the blood. The places where the fluids are made are in the glands. The process of making these fluids in the glands is called **secretion**. Some of these fluids serve but little use and pass more rapidly out of the system, and are generally called **excretions**. Thus the saliva, gastric juice, bile, and pancreatic juice are usually called secretions; for they are produced for a purpose, that of preparing the food. But the perspiration, containing as it does injurious elements resulting from the waste of the system, and being of use only to cool the body by its evaporation, is usually spoken of as an excretion.

The process by which food in a liquid form is taken into the blood through the capillary walls and through the lacteals is called **absorption**. The word is applied also to the accidental taking in of water or other liquid substances through the skin. Also we call that absorption, where one part of the body which is no longer of any use is carried away into the general current of the blood, as the gradual removal of the roots of the temporary teeth.

2. Perspiration. — A certain amount of water is constantly leaving the body through the pores of the skin. When the quantity is small, it evaporates as fast as it appears on the surface and we are not aware of the loss, but when it is more rapid and accumulates as moisture on the surface, we say that we are perspiring. When not sufficient in quantity to be perceptible to the eye, we call it insensible perspiration. The amount of insensible perspiration is much greater at some times than others, because when the air is dry and in motion, evaporation is much more rapid. The evaporation of the perspiration cools the body. This explains how our feelings or sensations are not a true index of the real temperature of the air; for when the air is dry and in motion, the evaporation is more rapid and we feel cool; and, on the other hand, although the temperature may be the same, if the air be moist and still, we feel very warm because the heat of the body is not carried away so fast. Strange as it may seem, a hot drink will cool the body, because it increases the perspiration, which by its evaporation produces a sense of coolness.

3. The Kidneys. — These are two important glands located in the " small of the back " behind the intestines. Their use is to remove from the body certain poisonous elements. They are generally spoken of as *excretory organs.* If their action be interrupted for any length of time, the person dies of blood-poisoning.

4. Absorption. — We have already spoken of absorption of the food from the alimentary canal, but this is not the only place where absorption may take place. Certain poisons are so powerful that if a drop be placed on the tongue a sufficient quantity is absorbed into the blood, and, affecting the nervous system, produces death in a few minutes. Some poisons are readily absorbed if merely rubbed on the skin anywhere on the body. If the epidermis be removed, absorption is very rapid from the surface.

Doctors sometimes apply " blisters," which raise the epidermis, and then apply medicines to the raw surface, that it may be readily absorbed. Tumors and unnatural growths sometimes disappear of themselves, the material being absorbed and carried out of the body as waste matter. A bath sometimes quenches thirst, because a sufficient amount of water is absorbed through the skin.

5. Waste and Repair. — You must constantly bear in mind that no part of the body is in a state of perfect rest. New cells are forming and old cells are disappearing. The material for the new cells comes from the blood, and the blood gets it from the food that is digested. This we call *nutrition* or *repair of the system.* The material of the old cells is thrown into the blood and carried away as matter that is no longer of any use. This is the *waste of the system.* Life seems to consist physically in this constant *waste and repair* of tissues. The body, then, is like a house upon which workmen are continually employed, removing old material and supplying its place with new material, thus keeping the house ever new.

LESSON 35.

Bathing and Cleanliness.

1. **Need of Cleanliness.** — We learned in the last lesson how foreign substances may be absorbed from the surface and poison the blood. *The excretions of the body, if again absorbed, act as poisons. Hence they should not be permitted to accumulate on the surface.* Besides, they cause dust and dirt to adhere to the surface and form a breeding-place for the germs of skin diseases of various kinds. *Cleanliness of person is a very important matter. Many diseases can be traced directly in their cause to want of personal cleanliness.*

2. **Value of Bathing.** — *The entire body should be bathed with water at least once every week, and under some circumstances every two or three days, or even every day.* In warm weather it is necessary to bathe more frequently. Occupations which expose the body to dust and dirt make it necessary to bathe often. Besides the need of bathing for cleanliness, it is frequently important to take a bath for curative purposes. *A severe cold may often be cured in*

*one night by a warm bath, but care must be taken not to ex-
pose the body to cold the following day or during the night,
as a more severe cold may be taken. In fevers lukewarm
or cool baths are valuable to lessen the unnatural heat.*

3. **How to Bathe.** — Where it is possible, a bath-tub in
which the entire body may be immersed is a great convenience and luxury, but it is not at all necessary to get
the full benefit of a bath. A gallon of water in any vessel, a sponge or soft cloth, and a towel are all that are
essential. *A thorough drying of the body by vigorous rubbing with a towel is important in cold weather.*

4. **Kinds of Baths.** — There are many kinds, as warm,
hot, cold, and lukewarm baths ; vapor baths, salt water
baths, shower baths, Turkish baths, etc. ; but for cleanliness the simple sponge bath as described in section 3,
with water of a temperature agreeable to the feeling
is as good as any. Cold baths are not advisable, as a
shock to the nervous system may result, which often
proves injurious. A hot-water bath and a vapor bath
always stimulate at first, but are followed by depression ;
and one should have a good rest afterward. Remaining
too long in the bath is not good, nor is bathing too frequently. Ten or fifteen minutes once a day should be
the limit.

5. **Clothing.** — We wear clothes to keep in the heat of
the body and to keep out excessive external heat. The
warmest clothes are those made from fur or feathers, and
next to these are woolen and silk garments ; next comes
cotton, linen being the coolest. *Wet or damp clothes
should never be worn for a minute, if possible to replace
them with dry ones.* If compelled to wear damp clothes

for a time, one should exercise to keep the blood circulating.

Clothing that is worn next to the body should be changed frequently, and if not washed every time should be well aired. It is better to have one garment to wear next to the body at night, and another in the daytime; then one will be airing while the other is in use, and at the end of a week, at furthest, both should be washed. Bedclothes should be aired every day and washed frequently.

6. Care of the Hair and Nails. — *The hair should be frequently combed and brushed* to keep the dirt from accumulating. Oil should not be put on the hair, unless it be unnaturally dry and harsh. *The finger-nails should receive careful attention every day.* The germs of disease are apt to appear in the dirt which accumulates under the nails. They should be carefully cleaned with a knife and nail-brush, with a little soap and water. Do not scrape the upper surface of nail with a knife.

LESSON 36.

The Brain and Spinal Cord.

1. The Nervous System. — We now come to study an important part of the body. It is that part that controls and governs all the rest, and is called the *nervous system.* The brain and spinal cord are the main parts of the nervous system, and form the subject of this lesson.

2. What is the Brain? — The brain is a large mass of nervous matter situated in the cavity of the head, and is the great controlling center of the nervous system. It is connected with the spinal cord and directly or indirectly with all the nerves of the body. Its average weight is a little more than three pounds, but there have been cases where it weighed four pounds. As a general rule, the larger the brain, the greater the mental power.

3. Coverings of the Brain. — There are three distinct coats or membranes which completely surround the brain, inside of its bony case. The outer membrane is called the **dura mater,** from the Latin, meaning "hard mother," the word *mother* being used in the sense of a protector. It is a firm fibrous membrane and serves as a *periosteum* to the bone as well as a protection to the brain. Next to the dura mater is the **arachnoid** membrane (spider-web-like). It is a very thin, delicate serous membrane. A space between the arachnoid and dura mater contains a serous fluid. There is also a space between the arachnoid and the **pia mater** (soft mother), which is the third or inner membrane. This covering consists of many minute blood vessels united by fibers. It is the nourishing membrane of the brain, supplying it with blood.

4. Parts of the Brain. — The brain consists of four quite distinct parts very unequal in size. Each of these again is double, that is, they are partly divided, by a fissure extending from before backward, into equal portions. These parts of the brain will be separately described.

5. The Cerebrum. — This is the largest portion of the brain. It fills all the space in the cavity of the head above the level of the ears. Looking at it from above, we get an appearance of many folds and furrows, as shown in the picture. The folds are called **convolutions**. They are more numerous in highly intellectual persons, fewer in the most intelligent animals than in the lowest races of men, and in the lowest quadrupeds the surface is almost smooth. The furrows which separate the convolutions are about an inch in depth. The object of the convolutions is to increase the amount of surface, where the important nerve cells are found. The under surface of the cerebrum is very irregular, a great many portions having been

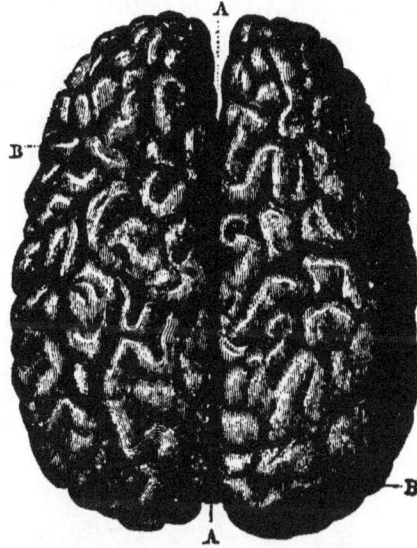

FIG. 20. — UPPER SURFACE OF CEREBRUM.

A, Longitudinal fissure; B, The hemispheres.

described under special names; but little is known of their special use.

6. **The Cerebellum.** — This is the next largest part of the brain. It is sometimes called the "little brain." It lies in the lower and back part of the cranial cavity. Its surface is marked by many curved furrows.

7. **The Pons Varolii.** — This term means "the bridge of Varoli," so named from an Italian anatomist. It seems to bridge together or connect the other parts of the brain.

8. **The Medulla Oblongata** (Oblong Marrow). — This is the pyramid-shaped portion which connects the rest of the brain with the spinal cord. It is the lowest portion of the brain, lying on the occipital bone.

9. The Interior of the Brain. — The brain consists of white and gray matter. These will be described in the next lesson. If the cerebrum be cut through horizontally about the middle, the cut surface will show on the outer edge a layer of gray matter following the furrows, and about one-fourth of an inch in depth. Next to this is a mass of white matter, and in the center is a peculiar-

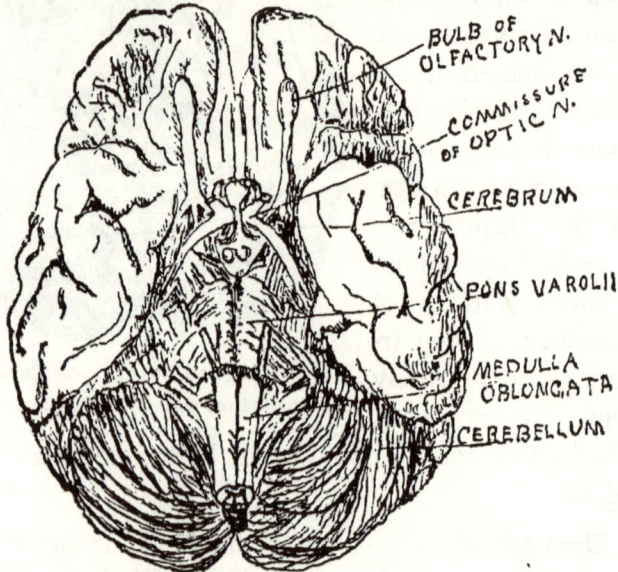

BULB OF OLFACTORY N.

COMMISSURE OF OPTIC N.

CEREBRUM

PONS VAROLII

MEDULLA OBLONGATA

CEREBELLUM

FIG. 21. — THE BASE OF THE BRAIN.

shaped cavity, one in each hemisphere or half of the cerebrum. These cavities are called **ventricles**. Besides these two large ones, there are three small ones, situated deeper in the brain. They are lined with a serous membrane and contain a watery fluid. Cutting through the cerebellum, we see gray matter on the outside and white on the inside, but so arranged that the white matter appears as a tree with many broad branches. This appearance is called the *arbor vitæ* (tree of life). The pons Varolii is a mixture of gray and white matter, and the upper part of the medulla oblongata has gray matter on the outside and white matter on the inside; but the lower has three kinds of nerve matter, reversed in position.

10. **The Spinal Cord.** — This is a long cylinder of nerve matter, that extends through the canal formed by the holes in the vertebræ of the spinal column. It reaches from the medulla oblongata to the lower edge of the first lumbar vertebra, or about the distance of sixteen inches. It is about one-half an inch in thickness. It is partly divided by fissures into two equal portions, and each of these again into two columns. The gray and white matters are arranged in a position the reverse of that in the brain; that is, the gray matter in the center and the white on the outside. It is covered by a continuation of the same membranes that cover the brain. At each vertebra a pair of nerves branch off.

LESSON 37.

The Nerves.

1. **What are the Nerves ?** — They are the white cordlike branches of the nervous system which extend to every part of the body, dividing and subdividing, somewhat as do the arteries and veins. So numerous are the small branches that there is scarcely a point on the surface of the body where you will not wound one or more by pricking with the finest needle. They are divided into two great classes : first, those branching from the brain and spinal cord, called the *encephalo-spinal nerves ;* and, second, those which form networks in the cavities of

the trunk and are only connected with the others by small branches; these are called *sympathetic nerves.*

2. The Cranial Nerves. — Twelve pairs of nerves branch off from the brain and are called cranial nerves. They are numbered in the order they leave the skull, beginning at the front. The names and uses are as follows : —

1. *The Olfactory,* or nerve of smell.
2. *The Optic,* or nerve of sight.
3. *The Motor Oculi,* or nerve of motion to the eyeball.
4. *The Pathetic,* also a nerve of motion to the eyeball.
5. *The Trifacial* has a branch to the tongue, being a nerve of taste. The other branches go to the eye and different parts of the face, and are nerves of motion and sensation.
6. *The Abducens,* a nerve of motion to eyeball.
7. *The Facial,* a nerve of motion to the muscles of expression in the face.
8. *The Auditory,* or nerve of hearing.
9. *The Glosso-pharyngeal,* a nerve of motion and sensation to the pharynx. It has a branch to the tongue, which is a nerve of taste.
10. *The Pneumogastric,* a nerve of motion and sensation to the lungs, stomach, and heart.
11. *The Spinal Accessory,* a nerve of motion and sensation to muscles of neck.
12. *Hypoglossal,* a nerve of motion to the tongue.

3. The Spinal Nerves. — From the spinal cord are given off thirty-one pairs of nerves known as spinal nerves. They pass out of the spinal canal from openings between the vertebræ, and are distributed to the trunk and limbs. They are all nerves of motion and general sensation.

4. Ganglia. — These are knots or little masses of gray and white matter in the course of the nerves. Thus, each spinal nerve has two roots, and on one of them is a ganglion. There are also ganglia on some of the cranial nerves.

5. The Sympathetic Nerves. — These are so called because they closely connect the various organs of the body

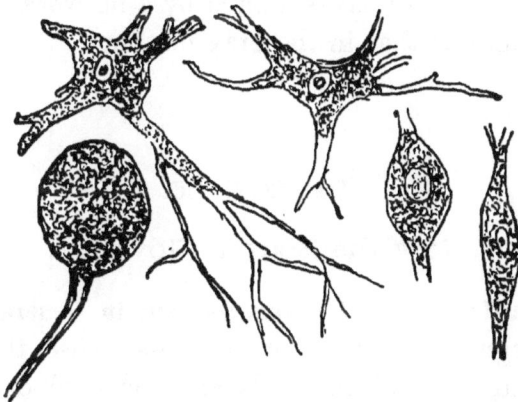

FIG. 22. — VARIOUS FORMS OF NERVE CELLS.

and are supposed to produce a sympathy of one organ for another, that is, if one organ is injured or diseased, other organs may be deranged also. The sympathetic system of nerves consists of two chains of ganglia, connected by nerves to each other and to the cranial and spinal nerves, and sending branches to the organs of the thorax and abdomen. These ganglia lie in front of the spinal column.

6. Structure of Nervous Matter. — All nerves and nervous matter consist of either *white* or *gray* matter or

both. The *gray matter* is found in the central part of
the brain, in certain large masses or ganglia at the base
of the brain, in the center of the spinal cord, and in the
ganglia. It is of a grayish or ashy color, tinged with
red. It is soft and pulpy, easily broken down by pressure
of the finger. It consists of a collection of cells em-
bedded in a fine network of fibers. The *white matter* is
found in the center of the brain, the outside of the spinal
cord, and composes the entire substance of the nerves. It
is, with some exceptions, of a dull white color. It consists
of numerous small fibers united by a network of fibrous
tissue similar to that in the gray matter.

LESSON 38.

How the Body is Governed.

1. The Use of the Nervous System in General. — Like
a well regulated factory or business house, the various
organs and parts of the body are governed or managed
according to a plan. Every part has its special work to
do, and they all work in harmony when in a state of
health. Thus, saliva is secreted in the mouth, and bile in
the liver, when the need for them exists in the stomach
and intestines. Strike at the eye, and the lid is quickly
drawn down to protect it. Touch the foot with a hot
iron, and quickly the muscles of the leg contract and
draw it away from danger. The general function or use
of the nervous system is controlling and governing the
body. This is brought about in three ways: *First,* a
peculiar activity we call *nerve force* seems to *originate* in
the cells of the gray matter. If these cells be destroyed,

all nervous activity at once ceases. *Second,* a power of *transmitting* or carrying this nerve force to and from the cells of the gray matter. This power lies in the nerve fibers of the white matter. Sever these fibers, and the part to which they are distributed has no longer power to act. *Third,* a power of receiving impressions from the world outside of the body. Thus, the retina of the eye receives impressions which inform us of the color, shape, and size of objects without touching them. The termination of the auditory nerve receives impressions we call sounds; and so on. Different nerve endings receive different kinds of impressions.

2. **The Special Use of the Cerebrum.** — The cerebrum is the organ of mind. It is that part which thinks and knows and wills or determines. You decide that you will stand up, or run, or sit down, or write, or work, or play. You could not do any of these without the cerebrum and be conscious of doing them. You might walk or write in your sleep, but you would have no knowledge of this action. The cerebrum is that which knowingly produces action. Animals will leap and walk and perform various actions when the cerebrum has been removed, but these are not conscious movements and are always produced by a stimulus of some kind, as when you jerk your hand away from a hot stove before you are conscious of its existence. This unconscious action is often called **reflex action.** Reflex action may be said to be motion without the use of the cerebrum.

3. **The Special Use of the Cerebellum.** — The cerebellum seems to be for the special purpose of controlling the muscular movements. A pigeon with its cerebellum removed seems to know what is going on around it and

what it wants to do, but is unsteady in its gait and misses
the food it pecks at.   It acts somewhat like a man who
is slightly intoxicated.   The man tries to walk straight,
but cannot, for he has lost perfect control of his muscles.

4. **The Nerve Centers.** — Most of the regular actions
of the body, as breathing, beating of the heart, etc., are
controlled by special nerve cells located in the medulla
oblongata.   Thus, in a frog, the brain may be all removed except the medulla, and the spinal cord completely
destroyed, and yet the animal breathes and its blood continues to circulate.   But if a certain point in the medulla
be destroyed, breathing and the beating of the heart immediately stop.   The medulla oblongata may be said to
be the great center of the nervous system, so far as mere
animal life is concerned.   The quickest way to produce
death in an animal is to paralyze the medulla.   Hanging
does this quickly by causing the axis vertebra to press
suddenly upon the spinal cord at the point where it joins
the medulla.   All gray nerve matter acts as nerve centers
where nerve force originates, but the great centers which
control the most important work of the body are in the
medulla oblongata.

5. **Special Use of the Spinal Cord.** — The white matter
of the spinal cord conducts nervous impressions from the
various parts of the body to the brain, and from the brain
to the various parts of the body.   Thus, if your great toe
strikes a stone, an impulse passes along a nerve until it
reaches the spinal cord, and from there it is conveyed to
the cerebrum, and you are conscious of the pain produced.
Yet all impressions do not reach the cerebrum.   For if you
touch the toes of a frog after its head has been cut off, it
will move as if trying to get away, perhaps even make

quite a leap; also, if you tickle the foot of a sleeping boy, he will move the leg, even though unconscious   In such cases we conclude that the gray matter of the spinal cord originates impressions which are sent out on the nerves, and causes the muscles to contract; and this we call **reflex action**. Another use of the spinal cord, then, is to act as a kind of secondary brain, impressions passing no further than the central gray matter of the cord, thus relieving the brain of part of its work.

6. **Advantages of Reflex Action.** — By having nerve centers besides those in the brain, the latter is relieved of part of its work, just as the head manager of a large business house need not give attention to many of the details of the business, but can have trusted overseers to look after the minor matters. When we have once learned to do any kind of mechanical work, we do it with very little thought. You do not have to think how you shall walk on a smooth road. You can even walk and be for a time unconscious that you are walking. So you can become so accustomed to writing that your pen will form the letters without thought on your part. In such cases the brain occupies itself with more important matters, and this kind of work is carried on by centers in the spinal cord. There is also a higher kind of reflex action, which may be called **automatic** ("self-action"). Thus we breathe and the heart beats, the glands secrete and the food is digested, all independent of the actions of our minds. It is very fortunate that such is the case, for if we were obliged to think and give attention to these matters, we might permit other matters to take their place in our minds, and we might forget to breathe or keep the blood circulating, and die from our own careless-

ness. The centers for such automatic action are in the medulla oblongata.

—•◦•—

LESSON 39.

Care of the Nervous System.

1. **Health of Other Organs.** — When one part of the body suffers, other parts suffer more or less. The nervous system cannot be in good condition without good blood, which nourishes it. There can be no good blood without proper digestion, circulation, and excretion. There must be a proper change of gases, — the reception of oxygen and throwing out of carbon dioxide; and this depends upon proper working of the respiratory organs. Therefore to have a sound mind one must have a healthy brain and nervous system, and *to have a healthy nervous system one must give attention to the rules of health pertaining to all the other systems.*

2. **Mental Excitements.** — The mind and body mutually act upon each other. Any disturbance of the nervous system affects the mind, and any powerful excitements of the mind affect the nervous system. Powerful "spells" of anger, excessive fear and grief, and even great joy disturb the nervous system, and through it the processes of digestion, secretion, respiration, and circulation. The nourishment of the nerve matter is thus lessened and the nerve tissue is injured.

3. **Mental Work.** — The nervous system is capable of accomplishing an enormous amount of work when the work is of a proper kind. Mere study and mental occupation are not injurious, unless very excessive. The mind

is always active during waking hours, even when we make no effort to employ it. You are always thinking about something, whether it be of importance or not; the heart continues to beat, the blood to circulate, breathing goes on; and all of these involve nerve activity. Even in sleep the mind acts partially. Dreaming is partial action of the mind. *It is not simply work, then, which injures, but misdirected and unnatural work.* All worry, excitement, and emotion are unnatural, and when long continued rapidly exhaust the nerve force. One needs a change of mental work, so that while one set of nerve cells are occupied another may be resting. In this respect the nerves are like the muscles.

4. **Sleep.** — During sleep all the powers of the body are renewed. *A proper amount of sleep is of the greatest importance, especially to the health of the nervous.* Children and old people require more sleep than others. Business and social matters frequently keep persons awake when they permit their minds to dwell upon them. We cannot control our thoughts except in one way, that is, we can avoid thinking of one thing by thinking of another. So, the best way to get to sleep is to think of as many different things as possible, — as it were, encourage the mind to wander from one thing to another. When it is concentrated on one thing, sleep will not come. *You can also avoid evil thoughts by trying to think of something that is not evil.* One should never take medicine for the purpose of causing sleep, without the advice of a physician. The proper time for sleep is during the hours of darkness. *Go to bed early enough to get all the sleep you need before daylight in the morning.*

5. The Effects of Alcohol on the Nervous System. — Alcohol acts on all the organs of the body by first deranging the nervous system. This disturbance of the nervous system naturally weakens and impairs it, and as a result a great many nervous diseases are liable to occur. Dr. Beard says: *" There is scarcely a nervous disease known to science that excess in the use of alcoholic liquors may not bring on or aggravate. General debility, neuralgia, insomnia (sleeplessness), epilepsy ('fits'), paralysis of every form and type, insanity in all its grades, as well as delirium tremens, may find in alcohol their exciting and predisposing causes." Worst of all is the effect on the mind. The moral powers become degenerated, and the man cannot control his appetite when the habit has been continued for a long time, and he becomes a confirmed drunkard.*

6. The Effects of Tobacco on the Nervous System. — *All young people are injuriously affected by the use of tobacco. It produces a tendency to nervous diseases of various kinds.*

7. Tea, Coffee, and Chocolate. — These drinks are not generally injurious to persons after thirty years of age, if used in moderation, but *their effects on the young are frequently as bad as that of tobacco and alcoholic drinks. Milk and water are the proper drinks for children and young people.*

LESSON 40.

Review of the Nervous System.

1. The nervous system is that part of the body which governs and controls all of the other parts.

2. The brain and spinal cord are the principal central organs or headquarters of the nerve force, as they con-

tain the gray matter, or that in which nerve power originates.

3. The nerves proper are the collections of fibers which
distribute the nerve force from the nerve centers in the
brain and spinal cord.

4. The brain and spinal cord are well protected by
three peculiar membranes, the inner one of which also
furnishes nourishment to their substance. What are the
names of these membranes?

5. The brain consists of four principal divisions. Which
is the largest? Which part connects the brain with the
spinal cord?

6. Name all the places where gray nerve matter is
found. How is the amount of gray matter increased in
the brain and yet exists on the surface?

7. The interior of the brain has certain cavities containing fluid. The use of these cavities is, doubtless, to lessen
the danger of shocks when the head strikes any object
forcibly. What do we call these cavities? How many
are there?

8. How does the arrangement of gray and white matter in the spinal cord differ from that in the brain?

9. All nerve fibers convey either power of motion, general sensation (as pain), or some special sensation (as sight,
hearing, etc.). The first are called motor fibers and the
last two are called sensory fibers. The spinal nerves all
have both motor and sensory fibers. The cranial nerves
are of three kinds; some contain all motor fibers, some all
sensory fibers, and others contain both motor and sensory
fibers. The eye, not even by the aid of the microscope,
can tell any difference between motor and sensory fibers.
We only know that if certain fibers be cut the power of
motion is lost in that part to which the nerve goes, and

if certain others be cut the power of sensation is lost in the part.

10. Although the brain is the great center of the nervous system, yet we suffer no pain if a portion of it be cut or bruised. There could be no pain without a brain, yet the brain itself suffers no pain. This is a curious fact.

11. "Heart-burn" is a peculiar pain in the region of the heart. It is caused by some irritation in the stomach. Sometimes the heart takes spells of "palpitating," that is, beating rapidly and irregularly. In such cases the heart itself is not impaired, but the cause may be sought in the digestive system. This unnatural action of one organ, caused by an irritation in another, is brought about through the nerves of the sympathetic system, which connects all the organs of the interior of the trunk. A severe blow on the abdomen, although it does not break the skin or rupture any of the tissues, may cause sudden death by the severe shock to the nerves of the sympathetic system.

12. Comparing the nervous system to a business house or great factory, what part would you say resembled the manager or head of the firm? Comparing the nervous system to a telegraphic apparatus, we can say the nerve cells of the gray matter are like the batteries which produce the electricity, and the fibers of the white matter are like the wires which convey the electricity.

13. What part of the nervous system is the seat of thought and consciousness? Could an animal with its head cut off suffer pain? What makes a chicken jump about after its head is cut off?

14. Explain how the mind and body act upon each other. Can there be a sound mind without a sound body? While it is true that some great mental achievements

have been made by men when they were suffering severely from disease, yet such mental efforts could not last long. The relations of mind and body are very close ones.

LESSON 41.

The Eye.

1. How the Eye is Protected. — You know what the eye is and what it is for, but perhaps you have never thought what a wonderful instrument it is and how well it is protected from injury. First, it is well surrounded by strong bony walls, called the **orbits**. Ordinary blows are received by the firm rim of bone in front, and nothing but a well-aimed thrust of a sharp instrument can affect the eye. Again, the orbit is much larger than the eye, and the extra space is filled with a cushion of fat, which lessens any shocks which would occur from falls or blows on the head.

The *eyebrows* shield the eye from excessive light and direct the perspiration aside. The *eyelids*, composed of cartilage and skin, act both voluntarily and involuntarily, closing instantly as danger approaches. Their edges contain glands which secrete an oily fluid which prevents the tears from overflowing on the face. The *tears* keep the surface of the eye moist and clear. The *eyelashes* shade the eye and act as feelers to warn of danger.

2. Where the Tears come from. — In the upper and outer corner of the orbit is a gland called the **lachrymal gland**. It secretes the fluid called **tears**. The tears are constantly pouring out through several little ducts upon

the surface of the eye. The frequent winking of the
eyelids causes the fluid to spread over the eyeball. At
the inner corner of the eye are two little openings, which
receive the fluid and conduct it to the lachrymal sac, from
which it passes into the *nasal duct* and through it into
the cavity of the nose. Here it evaporates, usually as
fast as discharged. When we weep, the amount of the
tears is excessive and they flow over on the face. The
surface of the eye and the inside of the eyelids are

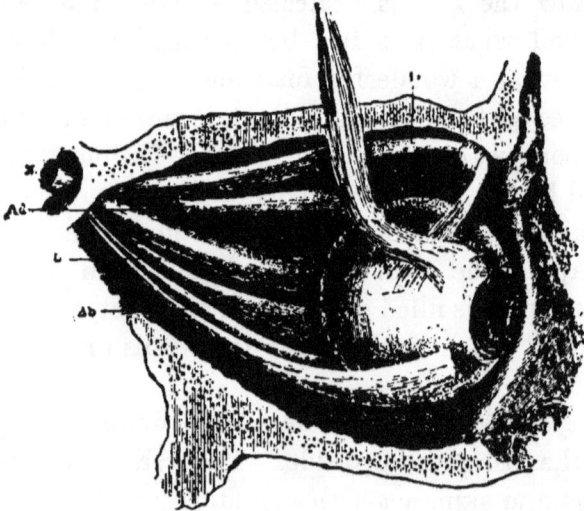

FIG. 23. — MUSCLES OF THE EYE.

covered with a thin, delicate mucous membrane called
the **con-junc-ti-va.** It is very sensitive and serves to
protect the eye.

3.   **Size and Shape of the Eyeball.** — It is about an inch
in diameter from side to side and from above downward,
but the diameter from before backward is a little greater.
It is like a sphere with a part of a smaller sphere placed

upon it. Six little muscles attached to the eyeball serve to turn it in all directions.

4. **The Coats of the Eye.**—The eye is composed mostly of membranes and transparent fluids. The outer coat consists of two parts, a transparent circular part in front called the **cor-ne-a**, which appears to fit like a watch crystal into the remaining part, which is called the **scle-rot-ic** coat. The part of this which we can see we call the "white of the eye." It is a very dense, tough membrane, elastic, but firm enough to give a globular shape to the eye. Just inside of the sclerotic coat is the **cho-roid** coat. It consists of a network of fine blood vessels and pigment of dark coloring matter. A little way back of the cornea is a circular curtain with a round hole in the center. It is called the **i-ris** and the hole is called the **pu-pil**. The iris is of different colors in different persons. When we speak of the color of a person's eyes, we mean the color of the iris. Just inside the choroid membrane is the retina, and the space enclosed by these membranes contains three transparent substances called, respectively, the vitreous humor, the crystalline lens, and the aqueous humor.

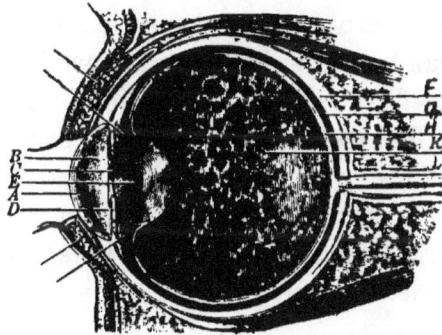

FIG. 24. — A SECTION OF THE HUMAN EYE.

A, Cornea; B, Aqueous humor; C, Pupil; D, Iris; E, Crystalline lens; K, Vitreous humor; L, Optic nerve; F, Sclerotic; G, Choroid; H, Retina.

5. **The Ret-i-na.** — This is the most important part of the eye, for it is no other than the expansion of the optic

nerve, which produces the sensation of light and vision. It consists of ten layers of variously shaped cells and fibers. One of these layers is called Jacob's membrane, and consists of numerous little rods and cones, which appear to be the real terminations of the nerve and the part essential to vision. These little rods and cones are not more than one ten-thousandth part of an inch in diameter, and it has been estimated that there are as many as a million in a space of one-tenth of an inch square.

6. **The Humors of the Eye.** — The transparent parts of the eye are called *humors*. Just behind the iris is the most dense of these humors. It is called the **crystalline lens.** It is a solid body, yet compressible and elastic. It is in the shape of a double convex lens, and is the principal means of converging the rays of light upon the retina. In front of the iris, between the crystalline lens and cornea, is a transparent watery fluid called the **aqueous humor.** The larger space behind the crystalline lens is filled with a thick, jelly-like, transparent substance, called the **vitreous humor.** These three transparent parts of the eye act as a compound lens, the purpose of which is to converge the light upon the retina, and form a picture or image of the objects from which the light is reflected.

7. **The Pupil of the Eye.** — This round hole in the iris is for the purpose of regulating the amount of light necessary to form the image on the retina. When the light is very bright, the pupil grows smaller; and when it is lessened, the pupil gets larger. This change in the size of the pupil is caused by muscular fibers in the iris.

LESSON 42.

How We See.

1. **The Eye is a Camera Obscura.** — If a small hole be made in the side of a box, and you hold it before some strongly lighted object and look down in the box, with your head covered with a cloth so as to shut out all light except what comes through the hole, you will see an inverted image of the object on the inside of the box. This is a **camera obscura** (dark room). If the hole be enlarged, it will be necessary to place a lens in the opening to converge the rays of light, or there will be no image. If the inside of the box be painted black, the effect will be much better. This is because the rays of

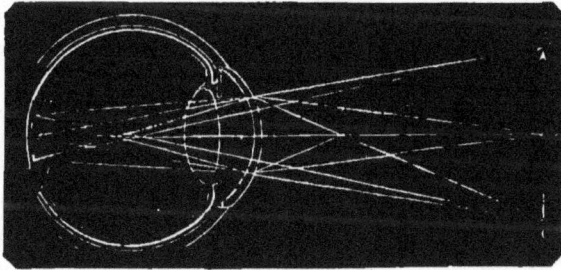

Fig. 25. — The Image on the Retina.

light which strike the sides of the box are absorbed by the black surface, and not reflected again on the image.

Now let us see how the eye compares with the camera obscura. The cornea admits the light to the chamber. The iris regulates the amount of light. The retina is the screen or surface upon which the image falls. The transparent parts of the eye form an adjustable lens, which converges the rays of light and makes the image fall upon the retina. The dark colored choroid coat absorbs

the indirect rays of light so that they are not again
reflected upon the image.

2. **The Picture on the Retina.** — The image or picture
which falls on the retina is, in some way difficult for us
to understand, conveyed to the mind so that we see the
objects which form the image in their proper position and
size.

3. **Accommodation.** — By this term is meant the adjust-
ing of the eye for distinct vision at different distances.
In the camera obscura, there must always be a certain
relation between the distances of the object, the lens, and
the image of the object.   In the eye there is no arrangement for changing the distance between the lens and the
screen which receives the image, but the crystalline lens
has the power of expansion, so that it becomes more convex; and this change in convexity
produces the same result as if a change
in distance were made, for the more
convex the lens the nearer its *focus*, or
the point where the rays of light form
an image.   This power in the lens
of the eye to change its convexity to
suit objects at different distances is
called *accommodation*.

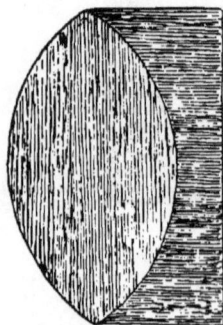

FIG. 26. — COMPOUND
LENS FOR CORRECTION
OF DEFECTS IN THE
IMAGE.

4. **Correction of Defects in the Lenses
of the Eye.** — In common lenses or
magnifying glasses, there is an indis-
tinctness of image and a slight amount of color in the
image produced.   In the most perfect instruments these
defects are corrected by using two kinds of glass in the
lens, of different degrees of density.   In the eye a similar

arrangement is seen, and the result is a perfect image of all objects.

5. **Near-sightedness.** — A perfect or normal eye can adjust itself for all distances beyond five inches. But there are some eyes in which the lens refracts too much, and the focus of the rays is not on the retina but in front of it, except when looking at very near objects. Such persons are said to be near-sighted. They can be enabled to see distant objects by wearing concave spectacles, which throw the image back to the retina.

6. **Far-sightedness.** — This defect in eyes is the opposite of near-sightedness. The person can see well enough at a distance, but not near objects. It is corrected by wearing convex spectacles.

7. **Old-Sightedness.** — This is not the same as far-sightedness, although the results are the same. In this case there is an inability to adjust the eye to near and far objects, and as the eye at rest is naturally adjusted to distant objects they can only see well at a distance. This occurs in old age, hence the name. Such persons must wear convex glasses when reading or examining near objects.

8. **Color-blindness.** — Some persons cannot distinguish colors readily, mistaking red for green, and so on. Such persons are said to be color-blind.

LESSON 43.

The Ear.

1. **The External Ear.** — The part we see projecting from the outside of the head, and which we usually call the ear, is comparatively of little use in man, as he can hear quite well if it be cut off. It doubtless aids a little in collecting the sound. It is composed of cartilage and skin. In the bottom of this part, which is called the **pinna,** is a tube which extends inward to the middle ear.

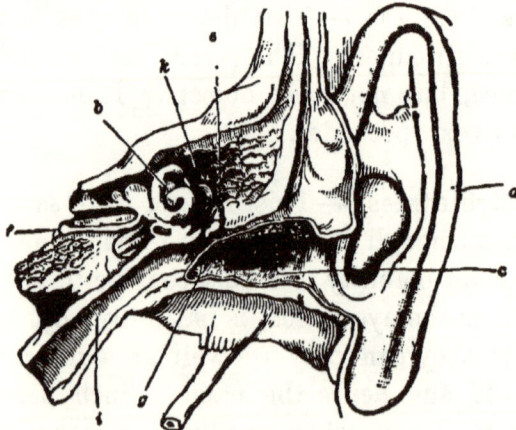

FIG. 27. — SECTION OF THE EAR.

a, Pinna; *b*, Semicircular canals; *c*, Auditory canal; *e*, Bones of the ear; *f*, Cochlea; *g*, Tympanic membrane; *i*, Eustachian tube; *k*, Tympanum.

It is called the **auditory canal**. It is partly in the skin and partly in the temporal bone, but is lined throughout with a thin skin which contains in its inner part glands which secrete the **ear-wax**.

2. **The Middle Ear or Tympanum.** — At the bottom of the auditory canal is an irregular cavity separated from

the canal by a membrane, called the **Tympanic membrane.**
A tube leads from the tympanum to the pharynx, called
the **Eustachian tube.** It permits air to enter the tympanum. The tympanum is lined with mucous membrane.

3. **The Bones of the Ear.**—Across the cavity of the
tympanum, extending from the tympanic membrane to
the opening of the internal ear,
is a chain of bones, not much
larger than heads of pins; but
they are very important aids in
hearing. The one attached to the
tympanic membrane is called the
mal-le-us (hammer). The one next
to this is the **in-cus** (anvil). The
next one joins the incus to the
internal ear, and is called the **sta-**
pes (stirrup). Although these
bones are exceedingly small, each
one is joined to the other by ligaments, cartilage, and
synovial membrane, the same as in other joints. They
move easily when a sound wave strikes the tympanic
membrane, and communicate the motion to the internal
ear.

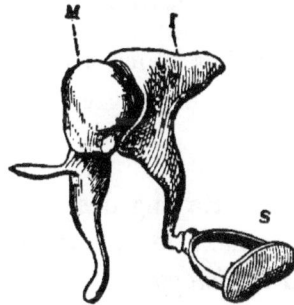

FIG. 28. —THE BONES OF THE EAR.

M, Malleus; *I*, Incus; *S*, Stapes. Enlarged.

4. **The Internal Ear, or Labyrinth.** — We now come to
describe the most important part of the ear, the place
where the sound waves are converted into impressions
made upon the nerve of hearing and, through it, upon the
brain and mind. The internal ear is a very curious cavity. It consists first of a cavity in the bone, which has
three parts, (1) the **vestibule,** or entrance, (2) the **semi-**
circular canals, three loop-like channels, and (3) the **coch-**

lea, a winding cavity very much like the interior of a
snail shell.   This curious cavity is lined with a serous
membrane, which secretes a fluid
called the **per-i-lymph.** In this
fluid floats a bag of membrane
which is nearly the shape of the
labyrinth.   This bag contains a
watery fluid called **en-do-lymph.**
The auditory nerve ends in
branches which are spread out in the labyrinth, one branch
ending in a great number of little rods called *rods of
Corti.*

Fig. 29. — The Labyrinth.

5. Having described the parts (*Anatomy*) of the ear, in
the next lesson we will explain the function of hearing
(*Physiology*).

———

Lesson 44.

How we Hear.

1. What is Sound ? — Sound is a vibration or wave
motion of matter, either solid, liquid, or gaseous, which is
capable of producing a sensation through the auditory
nerve.   Usually the sound comes to our ears through the
air, but air is not essential to sound or hearing.

2. Use of the External Ear. — The sound waves passing
through the air are conveyed through the auditory canal,
and strike the tympanic membrane.   The pinna in man
helps a little to collect the waves and direct them into
the canal.   In many of the lower animals it is very important.   You have observed how horses and rabbits, and

many other animals, turn their ears in the direction of the sound.

3. The Use of the Tympanic Membrane. — This membrane stretches like the head of a drum between the external and middle ear. When a wave of sound strikes it, vibrations are produced, which are communicated to the chain of bones. This membrane is very sensitive and vibrates easily when struck by sound waves. A tiny muscle serves to put it on the stretch and makes it more sensitive.

4. The Use of the Little Bones. — The tiny bones of the ear are nicely balanced upon each other, and being attached to the tympanic membrane they convey the motion of the membrane to the liquid of the internal ear, which is only separated from the stapes, or last bone, by a thin membrane stretched across an oval opening in the bony cavity of the tympanum.

The fluids and membranes in the labyrinth are set in vibration by the chain of bones, and this vibration affects the terminations of the auditory nerve. This nerve conveys the impression to the brain, and it is there received and produces in the mind the sensation we call sound. If you were to touch the auditory nerve, you would feel no pain, but would hear a sound. If you were to touch the optic nerve you would see a flash of light. These nerves have each a peculiar power.

5. The Eustachian Tube. — As mentioned in last lesson, this tube admits air to the middle ear. This is important, for, if there were not air on both sides of the membrane, it could not vibrate. It is necessary also that the air be frequently changed so that it may remain of the same density. Every time a person swallows, a little air passes up the Eustachian tube. It permits the mucus also to drain away from the tympanum. Also when there is a powerful sound and the membrane is forcibly pressed in, the air can pass down the tube and relieve the pressure.

6. The Use of the Ear-wax. — This peculiar, sticky, and bitter substance serves the purpose of keeping the ear clean and keeping out insects. It repels insects by its sticky and bitter nature and keeps the ear clean by catching the dust and drying up and falling off in scales, carrying the dirt with it.

LESSON 45.

Smell, Taste, and Touch.

1. The Nasal Cavities. — These are two irregular cavities in the nose. The openings in front are called the *nostrils ;* and those at the back, leading to the pharynx, are called the *posterior nares.* The bony walls of these cavities are very irregular and are covered with mucous membrane. These cavities serve to conduct air to the lungs and are the special seat of the sense of smell.

2. The Olfactory Nerve. — This is the special nerve of smell. It arises in the front part of the cerebrum and passes down through the ethmoid bone, there being about twenty branches which then spread out through the mucous membrane.

3. The Sensation of Smell. — Odorous particles of matter passing into the nostrils affect the olfactory nerve and give rise to the peculiar sensation of smell. These odorous particles must be in a gaseous state. If a perfumed liquid be placed in the nostrils and the air excluded, there is no smell.

4. The Organs of Taste. — The mucous membrane of the upper surface of the tongue, and the back part of the mouth, contain the endings of the nerves which give rise to the sense of taste. The **tongue** is a muscular organ covered with mucous membrane. On its upper surface are a number of little elevations called *papillæ*. These papillæ contain the terminations of the nerves of taste. Bitter substances are tasted most strongly by the back part of the tongue, sweet substances by the tip, and sour substances by the sides or edges of the tongue. A substance cannot be tasted unless it is in a liquid form. You taste sugar or candy which is not liquid, but not until the moisture of your mouth has dissolved the sugar.

5. The Sense of Touch. — The sense of touch is the power of distinguishing the shape, texture, and solidity of objects by contact with the skin or mucous membrane of the body. This power is much the greatest in the inner side of the ends of the fingers. In cases where the sight has been lost, the fingers become by practice much more sensitive. Blind persons are enabled to read by means of raised letters, and can tell quite accurately the form and texture of objects by the sense of touch alone. The nerves of general sensation in the skin have special terminations in the papillæ of the skin. These are supposed to be the special organs of touch.

6. General Sensations. — We speak of sight, hearing, smell, taste, and touch as the five special senses. Besides these we have other sensations, which may be called general sensations; among these is the *sensation of tempera-*

ture, by which we can tell within certain limits whether a body is hot or cold, warm or cool. Great heat or cold produces the sensation of pain. We are apt to be deceived by this sensation, for when an object is a good conductor of heat it carries away the heat of the body rapidly, and will when cooler than the body feel cooler than it really is, and when warmer than the body will impart its heat to the body and thus feel warmer than it really is.

Hunger, thirst, and fatigue are general sensations. *Pain* is a general sensation which is very useful to us. If it were not for pain to warn us of danger, we might be continually injuring some part of the body. We are able to judge of the weight of an object by holding it in the hands. This is not the same as touch, for we need not permit the object to come in contact with the body, and yet judge quite accurately concerning its weight or the amount of pressure it exerts. This is sometimes called the *muscular sense*.

———◦◦———

LESSON 46.

Care of the Sense Organs.

1. **The Eye** requires especial care if we would preserve its usefulness through life. *It is easily injured by dust, smoke, and irritating gases, overwork, insufficient or too strong light, and from other causes.*

2. *When some* **solid object** *gets into the eye, do not rub it,* for that causes further irritation. Make an effort to keep the eyelid open for a few seconds. The tears will accumulate and probably wash the object to the inner corner,

where it may be seen and removed. If this fails, blow the nose forcibly, at the same time closing the nostril on the opposite side. If these means fail, let some person roll the eyelid over a pencil and look for the object, removing it with the corner of a handkerchief.

3. *Do not put* **medicine** *in the eyes without the advice of a physician.* Bathing them with lukewarm or cool water will often relieve the irritation and do no harm.

4. *In reading or studying do not sit facing the light, but so that it comes over the left shoulder and falls on the book.* A lamp should be bright and steady. The electric arc light is too powerful for reading.

5. *Reading small type, on dirty colored paper and in a poor light is bad for the eyes. So is reading in a car or carriage when in motion, if continued any length of time. Do not read while lying down.*

6. The **eyes need rest.** They become weary by being used too long at a time looking at objects at the same distance. Whenever we look at a distant object, the muscles which adjust the eye are at rest, and when we look at near objects they are in a state of contraction. *When reading, one should frequently raise the eyes off the page and for a second or two look at some distant object. This gives the eye the needed rest. The eyes should not be used much when convalescing from sickness. They may be permanently injured in this way.*

7. **Tobacco smoke** *is injurious to the eyes, especially that of cigarettes. The bad effect of tobacco on the nervous system must necessarily affect the eyes to some extent. The eyes of the drunkard are never clear and bright, but blurred and bloodshot from the increased blood pressure in the capillaries.*

8. **The ear** is not so easily injured, perhaps, as the eye,

but certain rules should be observed in regard to taking proper care of it.   The ear is sensitive to cold winds, but the wearing of ear muffs is not to be recommended, as they are too compact and keep the auditory canal too warm, and thus render it more sensitive to cold when they happen to be left off.   A light shawl thrown loosely over the head should be used when the wind is strong and very cold.   A bit of cotton placed loosely in the ear is good in such cases.   In snowballing there is risk of snow being forcibly driven into the ear, causing serious trouble.

9.   The **ear-wax** should not be removed with an ear-spoon or any similar instrument unless unnatural in quantity or nature, and in such cases a physician should be consulted.   To keep the ear clean use only a wet cloth over the end of the finger.   *Never pick the ear with a pin, knitting-needle, or any similar instrument.*

10.   *Very loud sounds made close to the ear may cause deafness by rupturing the tympanic membrane.*

11.   Children sometimes are so foolish as to put peas, beans, cherry seeds, or the like in their own or a companion's ears.   In such cases they are often difficult to get out and may cause serious trouble.   There need, however, be no immediate cause for alarm, as the injury, if any, cannot come unless it remains a long time.   Turn the ear down and tap the head gently on the other side.   If it does not come out, use a syringe and a little warm water.   If these means fail, send for a physician who can extract it with proper instruments.

12.   The **sense of taste** is apt to be blunted by constant use of very highly seasoned and very hot foods and drinks.   The confirmed drunkard has lost the sense of taste in a great measure.

13. *All alcoholic drinks and tobacco have an injurious effect on the special sense organs, through their effects on the nervous system in general.*

—◦—

LESSON 47.

Alcohol and its Effects.

1. **What is Alcohol?** — Alcohol is a substance which does not exist in nature, but is the product of certain chemical changes on sugar. Under certain conditions of heat and moisture, germs of a microscopic plant grow and reproduce themselves in sugar, and convert the sugar into alcohol and carbon dioxide. This change is called fermentation. Sugar can in a similar manner be produced from starch. Therefore any substance containing either sugar or starch can by fermentation be used for the production of alcohol.

2. **Uses of Alcohol.** — Alcohol is a very useful substance *in its proper place*. It burns without smoke, producing intense heat. This makes it useful in many ways in the arts. It dissolves resins and oils, and is useful in preparing varnishes and paints. It hardens and preserves animal and vegetable substances, hence is useful to the microscopist and students of Botany and Physiology. In medicine it has many and important uses. Certain medicinal substances could not be extracted from plants without it; and, in a proper state of dilution, it is useful as a medicine in the hands of a skillful physician.

3. **Summary of the Effects of Alcohol on the Human Body.** — In the preceding lessons we have given brief

statements of the effects of alcohol on the various organs;
we here repeat them in a more compact form: —

1. *On the Bony Framework.* — The growth of bones is
checked by the injury done to the digestive and circulatory organs, whereby the supply of nourishment is cut
short. Dwarfs may be made of children by giving them
alcoholic drinks when quite young.

2. *On the Muscles.* — The power of muscles to act in
obedience to the will is impaired. The drunken man cannot walk straight, cannot talk correctly, and sees double,
because he cannot control the muscles used in these
actions.

3. *On the Digestive Organs.* — Alcohol has the effect of
removing water from the lining of the stomach and intestines, and thus tending to thicken it and diminish its
power of absorption. It hardens the liver and other
glands.

4. *On the Circulatory Organs.* — The blood vessels are
distended and overworked, in time. The heart is weakened by overwork induced by alcoholic excess.

5. *On the Respiratory Organs.* — The power of puri-
fying the blood is diminished, and the mucous membrane
of the respiratory organs is injuriously affected.

6. *It causes rapid loss of heat,* hence weakens the body
when it is exposed to great cold. It is a well-known fact
that among travelers, explorers, and soldiers, who have
been obliged to expose themselves to extreme cold, those
who were temperate stood the effects of the cold better
than those who drank.

7. *On the Nervous System.* — The power of the nerves
over the various organs of the body is weakened or disturbed; hence, through the nervous system, alcohol affects

all the organs of the body. It hardens nerve tissue and leads to insanity.

8. *On the Organs of Special Sense.* — By its general effects on the nervous system alcohol, when used for a long time, affects all the special senses.

Dr. N. S. Davis, a noted physician of Chicago, in a recent address said : " By all chemists, and other scientific men, it is classed as an active poison capable of destroying life when taken in sufficient doses ; and, if taken pure or undiluted, it destroys the vitality of the tissues with which it comes in contact as readily as creosote or carbolic acid. When largely diluted with water, as it is in all the varieties of fermented and distilled liquids, and taken into the stomach, it is rapidly imbibed or taken up by the capillary vessels and carried into the venous blood, without having undergone any digestion or change in the stomach."

4. **Social and Moral Effects of Alcohol.** — In a community where the drinking habits are not under restraint, the social and moral condition of the people is of a low grade. Drunken men are generally quarrelsome, and fights and murders are common where there is much drinking. A love of drink and its attendant amusements excludes higher and more intellectual sports and occupations. Alcohol, moreover, when used for a long time to excess, actually impairs a man's moral sense. It produces a kind of insanity peculiar to itself. When once a man becomes a confirmed drunkard, he rarely reforms. He may sign a solemn pledge and even exhort others to reform, but in spite of all inducements and persuasions of friends he is apt to return to his drink, having lost all moral power to abstain from it. *This should be a solemn*

lesson to those who have not formed the habit. The first drink leads to more, and the end may be a horrible one. Bad habits are nearly always formed in youth. If every one could be persuaded to abstain entirely from all intoxicating liquors and tobacco, until past thirty years of age, the probabilities are that there would not be one drunkard where there are now a hundred.

LESSON 48.

Tobacco and Its Danger.

1. The Extent of its Use. — There is not a race of people on the face of the earth that does not use tobacco. Thirty years ago it was estimated that 4,480,000,000 pounds of tobacco were used annually, and since that time its use has been increasing. This is no argument in favor of its value to the human race. The world might easily get along without tobacco.

2. Its Effects on the Human Body. — There are many persons who apparently are not affected by the use of tobacco. After middle age it often seems to be beneficial; at least, it is injurious in a less number of cases. It is undoubtedly injurious to young persons while the body is growing. The testimony of physicians and scientific men is almost unanimous on this point.

In many cases the chewing and smoking of tobacco causes dyspepsia of the worst form. In chewing, the salivary glands are excited when there is no food to be digested, and the saliva is thus produced in excess. The glands are thus weakened by overwork, and the quality of the saliva is impaired. Smoking tends to produce dyspepsia by its effects on the nervous system.

There is no doubt that tobacco injuriously affects the heart in a great many cases. Physicians recognize what they call a " smoker's heart" or " tobacco heart." It is a form of fluttering or palpitation of the heart, produced by the effects of tobacco on the nervous system.

On the nervous system itself, tobacco often exerts an injurious effect, producing sleeplessness, melancholy spirits, trembling, headaches, and sometimes disturbance of vision.

3. Slaves to Habit. — It is not good to become addicted to the use of any article of food, drink, or stimulant, to the extent of feeling that one cannot get along without it. Persons who get into the habit of using tobacco generally find it very difficult to quit it, and often find it hard to limit it in extent. The more one uses of any stimulant, the more the appetite demands. Persons who form habits of using tobacco and alcoholic drinks find themselves feeling miserable when, from any cause, they are compelled to be without them. This is certainly not a desirable condition. Young people should try to form habits of self-control of appetite. Appetite is a good thing, an essential thing, but, when perverted, becomes the ruin of the body and soul. **Learn to control your appetite.** The mind should be the master of the body, and not the stomach or the sensations. Herein lies the true pleasure of existence, the ability to control passion and appetite, and make them serve the uses of the body.

4. A Useless Habit. — *One who does not use tobacco feels just as well as one who does, and in most cases he feels better and enjoys life more. He does not, at least, feel the need of tobacco and he is saved the expense, which is no inconsider-*

able item.   Old persons who feel the need of a mild stimulant should use coffee or chocolate, and they will have no need of tobacco.

LESSON 49.

Other Stimulants and Narcotics.

1. Definitions. — Thus far we have discussed only alcohol and tobacco, among the substances classed as stimulants and narcotics. By stimulants we are to understand those substances which produce excitement or temporarily increase the forces of the system. Thus, alcohol makes the heart beat faster, the blood circulate more freely, and produces a temporary increased action of the nervous system; and we call it a stimulant. A narcotic is a substance which tends to depress or paralyze the forces of the system. All stimulants become narcotics when used in sufficient quantity or continued for a considerable time. *Stimulants add nothing to the strength, but simply cause strength to be exerted.* They are like the whip and spur to the horse. They do not increase his strength, but excite him to make greater effort, and the result is exhaustion comes the sooner.

2. Opium. — This is one of the most valuable of medicines when properly used, *but, when taken merely for its stimulating and narcotic effects, it is one of the most dangerous of drugs.* It is a kind of gum, being the dried and thickened juice or milk of a kind of poppy. It is grown chiefly in Persia, Turkey, and India. It is either chewed and swallowed, or smoked in a pipe. Its solution in alcohol is known as *laudanum*. Some who wish to get its intoxicating effect take it in this form. A white crystalline powder may be extracted from opium, and is known as *morphine*. It possesses all of the intoxicating properties of opium in a more condensed form. Many use morphine instead of opium.

3. **Effects of Opium.** — The first effects of opium is a pleasurable or comfortable condition of the entire system. Then a period of stupor follows and a disposition to sleep, in which there are usually very extravagant and sometimes frightful dreams. On recovering from the stupor, the body is weak, the head aches, and a very miserable feeling follows; and the victim of the habit is not happy until he has taken another dose. When the habit is once formed, the person is the most helpless slave imaginable. It is almost impossible for him to break off the habit. He loses his will power ; and, besides, the abstinence from the drug seems to produce a condition more miserable than the drug did in the first place.

In time the effects show plainly on the person. His skin becomes yellow, the eyes sunken and glassy, the body emaciated and bent, and the victim is a hopeless wreck of humanity. The moral sense is destroyed, and the person will not hesitate to lie and steal to get possession of his favorite drug.

4. There have been a few cases where men have cured themselves of the habit, simply by great will power ; but such cases are the rare exceptions. The people of Turkey, India, and China are especially addicted to the habit of eating and smoking opium. The habit is said to be greatly on the increase in the United States. The habit is a greater physiological crime than the use of alcoholic liquors, for it more rapidly gains control of the person, and

nearly always makes a physical wreck of the victim in a few years. Persons who suffer much from neuralgia, rheumatism, and similar painful diseases are apt to acquire the habit by using it freely as medicine. *No one should use morphine, opium, or laudanum without the advice of a physician; and even then it will often be better to suffer pain for a time than to take the risks of forming a habit of using these drugs.* Physicians are sometimes unintentionally the agents concerned in the formation of such habits.

5. **Indian Hemp.** — In India, Turkey, and Arabia large quantities of a resinous substance produced from the hemp plant is used as a narcotic. It produces a kind of temporary insanity, but does not seem to affect the circulation and digestion in such a degree as opium does.

6. **Coca.** — This is not the same as cocoa, from which chocolate is made. The latter is a comparatively harmless stimulant, while the coca possesses narcotic properties in the highest degree. It is the leaves of a bush which grows in South America. It is used by the natives of that country to a great extent. *Cocaine,* an extract from it, is now much employed in medicine.

7. **Betel-nut.** — This is the seed of a kind of palm-tree which grows in India and the islands of the Indian Ocean. It is chewed like tobacco and gives a deep red color to the saliva and to the lips and teeth. This is considered very ornamental by the natives. It is highly narcotic.

8. **Chloroform and Ether.** — These are two very valuable substances, used by surgeons to produce a state of insensibility while performing surgical operations. Since these substances have come into use, many important sur-

gical operations are possible which formerly could not be performed without great danger to life. Their proper use has saved thousands of lives, but there is no good thing that has not been abused by mankind. Many people, knowing the great relief from pain to be obtained by their use, have formed the habit of using them for every ache and pain; and some get into the habit of using them as others do opium for the intoxicating effects. *We would warn the young person who uses this book, to avoid all substances which produce stimulating and narcotic effects. Never take any of them without the consent of a physician.*

LESSON 50.

What to Do in Emergencies.

1. **Presence of Mind.** — The first and most important thing, in all cases of accident and sudden severe illness, is self-control on the part of those present. If one would just remember that screaming, crying, and rushing around madly does no good, but excites the sufferer and takes up valuable time which might be used in thinking what to do, and in doing it.

2. **Fire.** — If a person's clothes get on fire, seize any cloth or garment, as a bedquilt, a cloak, a piece of carpet, or a rug, and wrap him in it. If this be done fearlessly and quickly, the chances are that the fire will be smothered without serious injury to any one. Do not wait for water, as the fire is put out easier by smothering in this way.

3. **Fainting.** — Never raise a fainting person. The blood has left the head, and the prostrate position favors

its return. If one faints sitting in a chair, seize the back of the chair and pull it down until the head is on a level with the feet, or lower. This simple operation may restore him. Loosen the clothing about the neck and waist, and sprinkle cold water in the face. Keep away the crowd, as fresh air is very important. In apoplexy, however, the unconsciousness is due to rush of blood to the head. In ordinary fainting the face is always pale, but in an apoplectic fit it is apt to be flushed. An apoplectic person should be raised, the clothing loosened, and a doctor sent for at once. Apoplexy is not very common, and usually occurs to persons with short necks and of heavy build. It is most frequent in middle-aged or old people, and those who have been addicted to drink.

4. **Choking.** — Bits of bone or other substances sometimes become fixed in the throat and produce a troublesome cough or suffocation. In most cases a smart blow on the back between the shoulders will cause the substance to fly out. If this does not avail, look in the mouth. The object may be seen and seized with the fingers or a pair of pincers. An emetic of ground mustard and warm water may be given, if the person can swallow.

5. **Bleeding of the Nose.** — This often amounts to a serious trouble. Holding the hands and arms high above the head for several minutes has been known to stop it. The effort to do this causes the blood to flow more freely to the muscles of the arms and shoulders, and thus diverts it away from the nose. Bathe the face and neck in cold water. Pour a solution of alum into the nostrils. If these means fail, send for a physician. He will be able to stop it by properly plugging the nostrils.

6. Poisons and Poisoning. — It is not advisable to give here a list of poisons and antidotes, as the proper antidote would be very likely to be forgotten when the occasion required its use. But there are certain general principles to be observed which every one ought to know.

An emetic — that is, some substance which will produce quick vomiting — is always proper when poison is supposed to have been swallowed. The quickest emetic is a teaspoonful of ground mustard in half a pint of warm water. If this be not at hand, salt and water, warm water in large quantities, alum and warm water, or soapsuds may be used. If these fail, push the finger down the throat as far as possible. If nothing but cold water be at hand, drink copiously of it and then push the finger into the throat.

If the nature of the poison be not known, the emetic should be given first. If it is known, then the emetic is not improper if the proper antidote be not known or be not at hand.

All **alkalies**, such as concentrated lye, potash, sal-soda, and ammonia, are neutralized by acids. But only the harmless acids may be used, or they will produce their own poisonii.g if a little too much be used. The harmless acids that may be at hand are *vinegar, lemon juice, sour milk,* and *sour cider,* and possibly *cream of tartar.* Use these freely.

All poisonous **acids**, such as *sulphuric acid* or *oil of vitriol, nitric acid* or *aqua fortis, hydrochloric acid* or *muriatic acid, acetic acid,* and *oxalic acid,* require as antidotes the harmless alkalies. Those that are often at hand are *chalk, magnesia, soap,* and *lime water.* If nothing else be at hand, scrape the plaster from the wall, mix with water, and give.

After vomiting has been produced or the antidote given, it is proper to give any oily or mucilaginous substance, such as lard, cream, milk, white of egg, flour and water, or starch and water. These substances tend to prevent absorption of the poison from the stomach, and also soothe the irritation of the mucous coat. But, in case *phosphorus* is swallowed, *no oily substance* should be used.

7. **Sunstroke.** — This is a sudden prostration caused by long exposure to excessive heat, when the body has been weakened by fatigue or other causes. It may occur to persons who work in the house as well as to those who are in the sun. Most cases occur in large cities, where the heat is greater, and where there are more persons who are not accustomed to exercising in a heated atmosphere. It begins usually with dizziness or pain in the head, disturbed vision, and labored breathing, followed by unconsciousness. Sometimes it comes on very suddenly. The person should be carried to the nearest cool, shady place. Loosen the clothing and apply wet cloths to the head, and turpentine or mustard to the legs and soles of the feet.

8. **Drowning.** — A doctor should be called at once, but in the meantime the by-standers may do much toward restoring life. Remove clothing from face, neck, and chest. Place the person on the face, with one arm under the forehead. This position causes the tongue to fall forward, and permits the water to escape more freely. If breathing begins, proceed to restore warmth by applying hot flannels or cloths to the stomach, between the thighs, and to the soles of the feet. A little strong coffee or a little wine or brandy may be given. If breathing does not begin, try to induce it by turning the body on one side,

tickling the throat and nostrils with a feather or bit of paper, and dashing cold water in the face. If this does not succeed, turn the body back again on the face, supporting the chest on a folded coat or something of the kind; then turn back again on side, and repeat this operation for five minutes.

If by this time the doctor has not arrived, attempt artificial breathing by drawing the arms up over the head, then press them firmly against the side of the chest. Repeat this many times, while others are trying to produce warmth in the manner described. Persons have been restored after six hours of apparent death. So do not despair if good results do not appear in three or four hours of such work.

9. **Freezing.** — Do not take a person who is stupefied from exposure to cold into a warm room, but remove clothes if wet, and wrap in blankets, and rub the body vigorously with the hands, giving a little warm tea or coffee or weakened wine. Make him move about, if possible, and bend and move the limbs to increase the circulation. When extremities, as the nose, ears, or feet, are frozen, keep away from the fire and bathe in cold water or rub with snow. Then apply sweet oil or lard and wrap in flannel. Extreme cold produces a feeling of drowsiness. One should guard against this. To yield and go to sleep is certain death. Keep in motion as long as possible.

10. **Broken Bones, Dislocations, and Sprains.** — A broken bone may be known by the person not being able to raise the limb, by its bending where there is no joint, and by the pain and swelling; also by hearing the broken. ends grate on each other when moved. Place the person

in an easy position, apply wet cloths to the limb, and send for the doctor.

Dislocations are known by the unnatural appearance of the part, by the pain and inability to make all the usual movements of the limb. It is often difficult to tell the difference between a dislocation and a fracture. Send for a physician if either is suspected.

Sprains are sometimes more serious than fractures or dislocations. They are frequently very painful and long in getting well. Keep the limb quiet, and use warm and moist applications; warm vinegar and flannel cloths are excellent.

INDEX.

Note to the Teacher. — Pupils should be taught at a very early age the value of an index to a book. They should never for a moment think that it is the *text-book* they are studying, but the *subjects* therein discussed. There is no better way to impress this fact on their minds, and to get them out of the ruts of routine study, than to assign lessons in such a manner as to compel them to use the index. The teacher may occasionally select certain words from the index, writing them on the blackboard, leaving out the reference numbers, and require the pupils to find these words in the index, to look up the references in the body of the book, and to study them as a lesson. Practice in looking for words in an index and in finding the subjects in the text is a very important part of a pupil's training; for, as he goes out into the world and studies in libraries, indexes, dictionaries, and encyclopedias are his only teachers.

Note to the Pupil. — In studying lessons assigned you, if you find a subject not clear, consult the index of the book for the important words, and look up all the references there given. Some other part of the book may make the point clear, or a comparison of two or more paragraphs may help you very much to understand the discussion.

Atlas, 12.
Auditory canal, 128.
Auditory nerve, 110.
Auricles, 60.
Automatic action, 115.
Axis, 12.

Bathing.
　Kinds of baths, 104.
　Value of, 103.
Betel-nut, 144.
Bicuspid teeth, 33.
Bile, 45.
Bleeding, 78, 146.
Blood, Amount of, 70.
　Composition of, 70, 71.
　Circulation of, 102.
　Properties of, 70.
Bolus, 37.
Bones, Broken, 149.
　Composition of, 5.
　Covering of, 8.
　Growth of, 6, 7.
　Hygiene of, 14.
　Names of, 9.
　Number of, 9.
　Structure of, 5.
　Uses of, 8.
　Young and old, 6.
Brain, Coverings of, 106.
　Divisions of, 106.
　Location of, 105.
　Structure of, 108.
Breastbone, 11.
Breathing, 82.
Bronchial tubes, 84.

Camera obscura, 125.
Canaliculi, 7.
Canine teeth, 33.
Capillaries, 64, 69.
Carbonaceous foods, 52.
Carbon dioxide, 88.
Cardiac orifice, 38.

Carotid artery, 65.
Carpus, 13.
Cartilage, 7, 17.
Casein, 52.
Cavities of the heart, 60.
Cells, 2.
Cement, 34.
Cerebellum, 107, 113.
Cerebrum, 106, 113.
Cervical vertebræ, 12.
Children, 15.
Chloroform, 144.
Chocolate, 56, 118.
Choking, 146.
Choroid coat, 123.
Chyle, 48.
Chyme, 48.
Cilia, 84.
Circulation, Rate of, 74.
　Causes of, 73.
　Exercise and, 77.
　Cold and heat and, 76.
　Nervous shocks and, 77.
　Alcohol and, 78.
　Tobacco and, 79.
Clavicle, 11.
Cleanliness, 103.
Clothing, 104.
Coagulation, 71.
Coca, 144.
Coccyx, 12.
Cochlea, 129.
Cœcum, 41.
Coffee, 56, 118.
"Colds," 91.
Collar-bone, 11.
Colon, 41.
Color-blindness, 127.
Condiments, 56.
Conjunctiva, 122.
Convolutions of brain, 107.
Cooking, 54.
Corium, 96.
Cornea, 123.

THE END.

www.ingramcontent.com/pod-product-compliance
Lightning Source LLC
Chambersburg PA
CBHW020551270326
41927CB00006B/798